THE CAMBRIDGE FIRST CERTIFICATE COURSE

B. Gunputh

MICHAEL HINTON

ROBERT MARSDEN

JANE ALLEMANO

Nelson

Thomas Nelson and Sons Ltd
Nelson House   Mayfield Road
Walton-on-Thames   Surrey
KT12 5PL   UK

51 York Place
Edinburgh
EH1 3JD   UK

Thomas Nelson (Hong Kong) Ltd
Toppan Building 10/F
22A Westlands Road
Quarry Bay   Hong Kong

Distributed in Australia by

Thomas Nelson Australia
480 La Trobe Street
Melbourne   Victoria 3000
and in Sydney, Brisbane, Adelaide and Perth

© Michael Hinton, Robert Marsden and Jane Allemano 1988
First published by Thomas Nelson and Sons Ltd 1988

ISBN 0–17–555600–8

N.P.N. 9 8 7 6 5 4 3 2 1

Printed in Hong Kong

Designed and produced by the
Pen and Ink Book Company Ltd

Acknowledgements

**The publishers would like to thank the following for their
co-operation in producing this book. They have tried to
contact all copyright holders, but in cases where they may
have failed will be pleased to make the necessary
arrangements at the first opportunity.**

Kingston Careers Office for extracts from the *Kingston Careers
Service Handbook* on page 19.
The Office of Fair Trading for extracts from the leaflet *How to
put things right* on pages 69 and 70.
Vallentine, Mitchell and Co Ltd for the publicity blurb on
The Diary of Anne Frank on page 79.
Penguin Books Ltd for the publicity blurb on *The Secret Garden*
on page 79.
The Barbican Centre for the extract from the *Barbican Centre
Diary* reproduced on page 83.
The Controller of Her Majesty's Stationery Office for
permission to reproduce the adapted TV licence leaflet on
page 100.
The Consumers' Association for the article *Fear on the streets*
from *Which?* on page 112 and for the extract from the
booklet *Accidents and First Aid* on page 151.
The Evening Argus for the adapted *Spot the Ball* competition
on pages 124 and 125.
Checkpoint Books for material on page 140.
Acorn Computers Limited for the advertisement reproduced
on page 160.
Edward Vulliamy for his article on illiteracy printed in
The Guardian on 3 February 1987, reproduced on page 162.
Anglian School of English, The Brighton & Hove School of
English, English Immersion Courses, International House-
Northumbria, Sels College London and Wimbledon School
of English for information on page 162.
Berry Lipman/Selected Sound, Hook Norton/KPM Music and
Paul Ray/Parry Music Library for music on *The Cambridge
First Certificate Course* cassette.
Absolutely Stunning Songs for the song *Do it yourself* by
Horton/Mortimore/Austin, recorded live at El Fabuloso, 1986.

**Copyright photographs are reproduced by courtesy of the
following:**

Art Directors: 135; Associated Press: 102, 103; Barnaby's
Picture Library: 22; Anthony Blake: 135; J. Allan Cash: 127;
Colorsport: 127; Greg Evans: 120; Evening Argus, Brighton:
128; Rex Features: 102, 103; Forman Newspapers: 60; John R.
Freeman: 76; National Portrait Gallery: 76; S & G Agency: 120;
Sporting Pictures: 120; Chris Ridgers Photography: 123.

Illustrations by:

Chris Etheridge, Chris Hahner, Peter Joyce, Dave Parkins.

THE FIRST CERTIFICATE EXAM

The Cambridge First Certificate in English exam consists of five papers, which are described below. The exam has a total of 180 marks and you need about 100 marks to pass.

PAPER 1

1 hour

READING COMPREHENSION

Section A   Twenty-five multiple choice questions testing vocabulary and grammar.
Section B   Fifteen multiple choice comprehension questions based on three reading texts which may include visual information.

40 marks

PAPER 2

1½ hours

COMPOSITION

Two compositions on a choice of topics, such as a story, a description, a formal or informal letter, a speech, your opinions on a subject and questions on the set books.

40 marks

PAPER 3

2 hours

USE OF ENGLISH

Section A   A cloze test and language transformation items.
Section B   Information retrieval: A directed writing exercise based on your interpretation of information in a text such as a notice or advertisement.

40 marks

PAPER 4

about 30 minutes

LISTENING COMPREHENSION

Various types of questions to test understanding of spoken English, based on recordings such as a telephone conversation, a radio programme, announcements.

20 marks

PAPER 5

about 15 minutes

INTERVIEW

1   A conversation about a picture of some kind, followed by a more general discussion on topics related to the picture.
2   A discussion of short passages related to the theme of the picture.
3   A communication exercise (such as problem-solving, role play or discussion) based on some kind of realistic material (such as an advertisement or diagram). Or you can choose to talk about one of the set books.

40 marks

CONTENTS

INTRODUCTION TO THE STUDENT

Welcome to **The Cambridge First Certificate Course** which provides complete preparation for the First Certificate exam. It gives thorough practice in all the skills necessary to pass the exam and will help to raise your general level of English and your ability to communicate.

The Student's Book is divided into twelve units, which are each divided into three main sections: Language Study, Exam Focus and Activities.

The **Language Study** sections contain:

Vocabulary – words related to the topic, phrasal verbs and other words that may cause difficulties.
Verb review – the formation and use of all tenses, conditionals, passives, gerunds etc.
Grammar revision – structures not dealt with under Verb Review, articles, comparatives, etc.
Speech work – stress, intonation and pronunciation.
Functions – the most common language functions, such as greetings, giving advice, asking for information.

The **Exam Focus** sections give descriptions of all the examination papers and question types, with advice on how to approach them. In addition, some aspect of composition writing is dealt with in every unit.

The **Activities** sections contain authentic reading texts, listening tasks, discussions, role plays, communicative activities and games.

Progress Tests are provided after Units 3, 6, 9 and 12, with exercises in the examination format.

At the back of the book you will find the tapescripts, an appendix of useful information and an index.

EARNING A LIVING

LANGUAGE STUDY

Vocabulary

What are the names of these jobs?
Which would you like to do?

Word families: work

Examples

a I'm looking for a *job*.

b I'm looking for *work*.

c Each day our teacher sets us a new and demanding *task*.

d The government's aim is to create full *employment*. ~has a job~

e Cox retired at the age of 73, after a lifelong *career* in the Navy.

f 'Name?' asked the policeman. 'Mary Johnson,' I said. *'Occupation?'* 'Plumber.'

g He was tired of working for others, so he went into *business* on his own.

h He is not strong enough to do anything involving heavy manual *labour*. ~buy selling~

i France hopes to increase its *trade* with Japan.

j Our Member of Parliament is a teacher by *profession*.

~homework~

A Find words from the examples above to fill each gap. Then try to line up the answers correctly in the word square, so as to make a three-word phrase down the centre that means *unemployed*. Two words have been done for you.

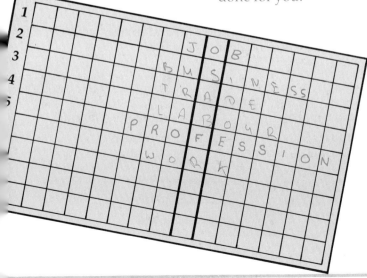

1 My ___job___ is to make the tea.
2 There are great financial risks in going into ___business___
3 Britain's overseas ___trade___ has declined in recent years.
4 The murderer was sentenced to ten years' hard ___labour___.
5 Just now I'm working as a writer, but I'm a doctor by ___Profession___
6 I always get to ___work___ at 8.
7 The bank manager wanted to know her name, her age, and her ___occupation___
8 He was a promising politician, but a series of scandals ruined his ___career___.
9 Right! Your next ___task___ is to cross the river without getting wet.

Phrasal verbs: *get*

B   Match the phrasal verbs with the definitions. The first has been done.

4	get away	4
5	get away with (something)	☐
9	get by	☐
6	get (it) over with	☐
8	get on	☐
7	get on with (someone)	☐
3	get on with (something)	☐
	get out of (something)	☐
11	get over (something)	☐
1	get through	☐
2	get together	☐
10	get up to (something)	☐

1 achieve a connection, usually by phone
2 collect in one place, meet
3 continue
4 depart, leave
5 escape or avoid (a duty or obligation)
6 finish (something unpleasant)
7 have a friendly relationship
8 make progress
9 manage or cope adequately but not easily
10 plan, be involved in (usually mischief)
11 recover from (something)
12 succeed in doing (something) unpunished

C   Fill each gap with one of the above phrasal verbs.

1 How can I _get out_ going to the annual general meeting?
2 No one should be allowed to _get away_ with such terrible behaviour.
3 It took him many months to _get over_ losing his job.
4 He'll always be successful because he _get on with_ his superiors so well.
5 He's _getting on_ well. I'm sure he'll be company director soon.
6 He hardly earns enough money to _get by_.
7 I wonder what she's _getting up to_ these days. Planning something, I expect.
8 We must _get on with_ our work. Drinking coffee doesn't earn money.
9 I've been trying to phone New York all morning, but I can't _get through_.
10 Give me the bad news first, and _get it over_.
11 I haven't seen you or your wife for ages. Let's _get together_ at the weekend.
12 If I'm going to catch that plane, I'll have to _get away_ by nine o'clock.

Verbs easily confused: *make* and *do*

*You **do** the cooking but you **make** a cake.*

Put *make* or *do* in these rules.

General rules:
  a) _do_ = carry out an action or task
  b) _make_ = create or construct, and is followed by a word showing the *result* of an activity or task
  c) There are so many exceptions to rules (a) and (b) that you will have to learn every use of *make* and *do* individually.

D   Using your dictionary to help you, write *make* or *do* beside each phrase. Then write sentences of your own containing each expression.

_____ an excuse	_____ someone a favour
_____ the shopping	_____ your duty
_____ the cleaning	_____ an attempt
_____ a suggestion	_____ the housework
_____ a noise	_____ plans
_____ a profit	_____ a bed
_____ a mistake	_____ trouble
_____ damage	_____ war

Verb review: the present simple and present continuous

Formation of regular verbs

Complete the gaps in the tables below.

Present simple		
+	**–**	**?**
I work.	You _____	Do they work?
He _____	He does not work.	_____ she work?
Contractions:		
	You _____	_____ you work?
	He doesn't work.	_____ he work?

Notes
● Verbs that end with *y* preceded by a consonant, change the *y* to *ies* in the third person singular: *I worry – He worries* (but *I pay – He pays*).
● Verbs that end with -*ss*, -*sh*, -*ch*, -*x* add -*es*: *I pass – He passes.*

Present continuous		
+	**–**	**?**
I _____	I am not working.	_____ they working?
You _____	You are not working.	_____ you working?
He is working.	She _____ working.	Is she working?
Contractions:		
I'm working.	I'm not working.	Aren't I working?
You _____	{ You aren't working. { You're not working.	_____ you working?
He _____	{ He isn't working. { He's not working.	_____ he working?

Notes
● Verbs that end in silent *e* drop the *e* when -*ing* is added: *bite/biting*.
● A final consonant (except *w*, *x*, and *y*) is doubled before -*ing* if the preceding vowel is stressed and spelt with a single letter: *put/putting*.
● In British English, verbs that end with a single *l* after a vowel spelt with a single letter always double the *l*: *travel/travelling*.

Use of the present simple and present continuous

The **present continuous** refers to time periods of limited duration, where a change in the situation is expected at some time in the future. It is often associated with phrases such as: *(just) now, at this moment.*

I'm working in London. (A limited time period. The situation is temporary; at some time in the future I may work elsewhere.)

The **present simple** refers to unlimited time periods, particularly with habitual actions (*I start work at nine*) and general truths (*The sun rises in the east*). Commonly associated phrases are those that answer the question 'How often?': *always, often, usually, every day,* etc.

I work in London. (An unlimited time period. I see this as a permanent situation.)

A What are the *-ing* forms of these verbs?

apply, begin, chop, delete, forget, level, listen, make, tax, try

What are the infinitive forms of these verbs?

labelling, batting, dining, referring, compelling, polling, probing, regretting, scoring, sniping

B Match up **a** and **b** with the sentence endings by putting **a** or **b** in each box.

a *I drink coffee _____*

1 [b] at the moment.
2 [a] when I can't find any tea.
3 [a] every morning.
4 [b] in order to stay awake for tomorrow's exams.
5 [b] but I usually drink tea.

b *I'm drinking coffee _____*

6 [b] all the time.
7 [b] because I can't find any tea.
8 [b] even though I've never drunk it before.
9 [a] three times a day.
10 [a] whenever I'm thirsty.

C Guessing game

Work in pairs. Each student chooses a job. Find out what your partner's job is by asking yes/no questions about his or her routine, like this:

Do you work outside? Do you wear a uniform? etc.

When you have found each other's jobs, imagine that you are swapping jobs just for today, in order to find out what the other job is like. Write five sentences describing differences between the two jobs, like this:

I usually work outdoors, but today I'm working indoors.
Normally I spend a lot of time meeting people, but today I'm working on my own.

Give your sentences to someone from a different pair. Can he or she guess what your normal job is and what your temporary job is?

D Make up dialogues about the people in the pictures, like this:

What does Brian Jenkins do? – He's a chef.
What's he doing at the moment? – He's frying an egg.

Brian Jenkins

Eileen Collins

Jim Nicholson

Paula Reed

Doris Chetty

Alex Parker

Simon Hill

Notes

● The **present continuous** is also used with repeated or habitual actions to express irritation or anger, particularly with the word *always*:

You're always asking me difficult questions. Ask your teacher instead.

● The present continuous is not normally used with verbs related to:
  a) passive use of the senses (*hear, see, smell, taste*). *Can* is used instead to express a temporary, 'present continuous' meaning:

  I usually hear very badly, but you are speaking so clearly that I can hear every word.

  But verbs that describe active, deliberate use of the senses *are* used with the present continuous (*listen, look, watch*):

  I'm looking very hard, but I can't see anything.

  b) emotions (*care, forgive, hate, like, refuse, want, wish*)
  c) beliefs and understanding (*expect, know, realise, remember, understand*)
  d) possession (*belong, own, possess*)
  e) various other verbs (*consist, contain, matter, seem*)

E Make up as many sentences as you can about the man in the picture and his life, using verbs from the lists in the *Notes* above. For example:

  He hates the noise.
  He can see a block of flats in the distance.

Grammar revision: countables and uncountables

Countable nouns are those which are seen as individual items which can, literally, be counted. For example: *dog* (*one dog, two dogs*, etc.)

Uncountable nouns cannot be counted. They are seen as a mass which cannot be separated. Examples: *tea, bread, news, anger.*

A Show which nouns are countable and which are uncountable by putting the indefinite article *a* before the countable nouns.

It was:

_____ *very bad behaviour.* u   _____ *very helpful suggestion.* u
_____ *very fine weather.* u   _____ *very ugly furniture.* u
_____ *very good advice.* u   _____ *very intelligent remark.* c
_____ *very hard homework.* u   _____ *very useful information.* u

B Choose the correct words to complete the following sentences. Some sentences have more than one correct answer.

1 They've just bought some very nice _____.
   A chair   B chairs   C furniture

2 Every _____ in the shop was damaged.
   A chair   B chairs   C furniture

3 I'm not sure that we've got enough _____.
   A chair   B chairs   C furniture

4 I think she's got a few _____ left.
   A apple   B apples   C fruit

5 We've got so little _____ that I'll have to go shopping.
   A apple   B apples   C fruit

6 This _____ is not yet ripe.
   A apple   B apples   C fruit

7 Don't buy any _____! Far too expensive!
   A cup of tea   B cups of tea   C tea

8 In the village hall, they were serving _____ and biscuits.
   A cup of tea   B cups of tea   C tea

Nouns which are countable and uncountable

Some nouns are countable in one sense and uncountable in another.

*The sun gives **light** and heat.* (uncountable – the opposite of darkness)
*Turn on all the **lights**.* (countable – objects which produce brightness)

C Make pairs of sentences to show these words used as
(a) uncountables and (b) countables:

cake, difficulty, experience, glass, lamb, paper, sound, speech, stone, winter

Uncountable nouns are often made countable by the addition of phrases:

*I heard two interesting **bits of** news.*
*I ate five **pieces of** bread.*

D Fill the gaps with suitable phrases based on the words in the box.

1 I had a _work of_ good luck.

2 The boys broke two _pane of_ glass.

3 She sold six _stroke_ art by Dali.

4 He ate three _bar of_ chocolate.

5 I thought I felt a _drop_ rain.

6 We drank two _cup of_ coffee.

7 I tore up five _sheet of_ paper.

8 Give him a _around_ applause!

9 No _act of_ violence, please.

10 Then add a _pinch of_ salt.

act	pinch
bar	round
cup	sheet
drop	stroke
pane	work

Speech work: word stress

A   Every English word has a fixed stress pattern. Listen to these words on tape and mark the stressed syllables, as in the examples. Then practise saying the words aloud, emphasizing the stress patterns.

camping   revenge   printer   handsome   believe   massive   person
haunted   entice   cupboard   mercy   teacher   student   reflect
sailor

B   In unstressed syllables, vowel sounds are usually shortened. Listen to the words in exercise A again, concentrating on the unstressed syllables. Sort the words into two lists:

A (unstressed syllable pronounced /ə/, as in *a*bout)	**B** (unstressed syllable pronounced /ɪ/ as in sit)

A good dictionary will indicate which syllables are stressed, and which vowels are weakened. You should get into the habit of learning the stress pattern every time you learn a new word.

C   There is a large group of words in which the position of the main stress depends on the part of speech. Listen to these words and say them aloud.

Nouns: object   permit   contest   progress   record

Verbs: object   permit   contest   progress   record

Now work in pairs. Say one of the words to your partner. Can he or she hear if it is a noun or a verb?

D   Write ten sentences of your own, using the words in Exercise C as nouns and verbs. Then practise reading your sentences aloud.

Functions: asking for permission and making requests

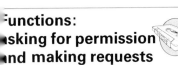

Employee: Could I possibly have the morning off tomorrow to go to the dentist?
Employer: Of course. By the way, I've got something to ask you. Would you mind working late tonight? We must get this report finished.
Employee: Certainly, I can stay as late as you like.

A   Decide which phrases in the dialogue above could be replaced by the following expressions. Then practise reading the dialogue aloud, using the alternatives.

Is it all right if I _possibly_?
Do you mind if I _morning_?
Would it be possible to _____?

Would you please _mind_?
Would you be so kind as to _____?
Could you _work_, please?

B   In pairs, take the parts of employee and employer in these situations:

The employee wants permission to:
● change holiday dates
● have an advance on pay
● make a private phone call

The employer wants him/her to:
● write an extra report
● show a visitor around
● deliver a package on the way home

EXAM FOCUS

Paper 1, Section A: vocabulary

This section consists of 25 questions, each of which is a sentence with one word or phrase missing. You have to fill the gap by writing the letter of the best alternative. e.g. 1B.

The questions are designed to test various aspects of English, including:

Type 1 words which are followed by a particular preposition:

He spend ages _____ at the trains.
A listening   B looking   C regarding   D watching

Type 2 idiomatic usage (i.e. words which are always used together):

They couldn't go out because of the _____ rain.
A bad   B fast   C heavy   D strong

Type 3 meaning – only one word fits the meaning of the sentence:

I advise you to _____ it, in case he sees it.
A offer   B display   C hide   D show

Type 4 grammar:

That old house is at last _____ down.
A been knocked   **B** being knocked   C knocking
D knocks

to get to get down

Type 5 phrasal verbs:

The boy took a long time to get _____ his illness.
A off   B out of   C over   D through

Dos and don'ts

● Don't choose until you understand the meaning of the sentence completely.
● Look very carefully at the sentence, particularly the structure and prepositions. Often more than one word will fit the meaning, while only one will fit the structure.
● Be observant whenever you listen to and read English, so as to increase your knowledge of idiomatic usage (how words normally go together).
● Never leave a blank. If you don't know the answer, make a guess.

Choose the best words or phrases to complete the sentences. Then categorise each sentence according to the groups above.

1 It takes me an hour every morning just to get _____ my mail.
A away   B into   C over   D through

2 The answer was on the _____ of my tongue.
A edge   B end   C point   D tip

3 I wish I had applied _____ that job.
A at   B for   C of   D to

4 I can never find shoes to _____ me – my feet are so narrow.
A fit   B go   C match   D suit

5 There are _____ people out of work in Sweden than in Britain.
A few   B fewer   C less   D little

6 His job _____ of interviewing the public and writing reports.
A consists   B contains   C includes   D involves

Composition: Introduction

Paper 2 (Composition) usually contains five questions, of which you have to answer two. Questions will probably belong to these categories:

- *a letter* — either informal (e.g. to a friend or relative) or formal (e.g. to an employer, a bank manager, etc.)
- *a narrative* — making up a story, usually about yourself
- *a description* — of a person, object, place or event
- *a speech* — writing down the actual words you would speak in a given situation (formal or informal)
- *a discussion* — giving your opinions on the rights and wrongs of a topic
- *'set books'* — a question on the books set by the examiners that candidates may prepare in advance if they wish. There is usually one question about each book.

In this book you will find advice and practice for all these composition types *except* the set books.

Dos and don'ts

- Read each question very carefully. You must answer the question exactly as it is formulated. You will lose marks if you miss part of the question or if you alter the situation.
- Decide on the style needed. Use *informal* language for writing or speaking to friends or relatives. Otherwise use *formal* language, particularly in discussion essays and non-dialogue parts of narratives and descriptions.

A   For each point of style write **I** or **F** in the boxes to show which is formal and which is informal. One has been done for you.

contractions (*can't, I'm*) [I]	standard words (*depart*) [F]
full forms (*cannot, I am*) [F]	colloquial expressions (*get away*) [I]

indirect questions (*I wonder if you know what his name is?*) [F]	
direct questions (*What's his name?*) [I]	abbreviated words (*plane*) [I]
	full forms (*aeroplane*) [F]

exclamation marks (!) [I]	fillers (*well, ah*) [I]
no exclamation marks [F]	no fillers [F]

How many examples of the above points of style are there in the following extracts from letters? Which letter is formal and which is informal?

It was great to see you again the other day. I can't believe it has been so long since we last saw you.
Anyway, I'm writing to ask you a favour. Could you possibly send me a copy of that job advert you were talking about? It looked just up my street, but I can't find it anywhere in my paper.

I was interested to read your advertisement in the local newspaper for the post of computer programmer. I would be grateful if you would send me further details and an application form.

Answering the questions

Look at this example of a typical composition question.

During the summer you stayed with some English friends for a few weeks. Write a letter to them thanking them and telling them what you have been doing since you saw them.

The best way to start is to ask yourself the questions **a–e** below. The answers (for the above example) are given.

Questions	*Answers*
a What kind of composition is it?	A letter
b How many sections does the question ask for?	Two – saying 'thank you' and saying what you have been doing
c What style is needed?	Informal – it's a letter to friends
d What are the key words in the question?	*Summer – stayed with English friends – a few weeks – thanking – doing since you saw them*
e Is there any language in the title that it would be natural to use in the composition?	Yes – notice the tenses: *During the summer you stayed . . .* and *you have been doing since you saw them*. It would be natural to base the first section of your answer on the first of these phrases (*I had a lovely time when I stayed with you during the summer*) and the second section on the second phrase (*Since I saw you, I have been visiting etc.*)

B   Read the composition questions carefully. Then answer questions a–e above for each composition.

1 You were sitting at home one day when you heard a loud explosion outside. Describe what happened next.

2 Is there any cause for people to be worried about nuclear power?

3 A new student has arrived at your college and has asked you about the college's timetable and facilities. Write what you would say to him/her

4 You have been <u>offered</u> a place at a college for next year, but you are unable to take up the place. Write to the principal explaining why and asking for a place for the following year.

untant	Ambulance driver	Architect	Armed services	Art teacher
r	Bank clerk	Banker	Beautician	Book keeper
ding trades	Butcher	Cameraman/	Cashier	Chef
engineer	Clerk	woman	Computer operator	Computer programmer
y typist	Cosmetics demonstrator	Commercial artist	Dentist	Dietician
tor	Draughtsman/woman	Dental technician	Estate agent	Farm manager
n worker	Fireman/woman	Dressmaker	Food technologist	Gardener
phic designer	Hairdresser	Florist	Hospital administrator	Hotel manager
me tax inspector	Interior designer	Home help	Mathematician	Midwife
del	Motor mechanic	Librarian	Nurse	Optician
sonnel officer	Pharmacist	Museum assistant	Photographer	Picture restorer
ot	Policeman/woman	Physiotherapist	Postman/woman	Printer
bation officer	Psychologist	Porter	Riding instructor	Sewing machinist
op assistant	Shorthand typist	Receptionist	Speech therapist	Surveyor
ephone engineer	Telephonist	Social worker	Travel clerk	Veterinary surgeon
aiter/waitress		Traffic warden		

nterview

t people find interviews a bit nerve-
ing, but there are two things you can
r in mind which may help to build your
fidence.

stly, an interview is a two-way process – it
es you the opportunity to ask about the
and see if it's right for you, as well as
ing the interviewer's chance to find out
re about you and whether or not you are
table for the job.

econdly, employers will very often follow a
nd of checklist when they are interview-
g, and if you bear in mind what they will
ant to know you can ensure that you are
roperly prepared.

Here are some comments made by local
employers about interviews they have conducted. Try and make sure you avoid their
criticisms by following the advice in the
right hand column.

Which category best suits you?

☐ *Scientific* – are you interested in knowing how and why things work?

☐ *Social* – are you interested in caring for others and helping them with their problems?

☐ *General service* – would you like a job which involves offering a service to other people?

☐ *Artistic* – would you like to use artistic or creative abilities?

☐ *Computational* – do you have an aptitude for working with figures or solving mathematical problems?

☐ *Practical* – do you like making things with your hands or with machines?

☐ *Nature* – are you interested in working with plants or animals?

☐ *Outdoor/active* – would you like to be out and about and physically active?

WRONG
"Arrived late"

"Looked scruffy" unhidety

"Didn't seem interested" interesting

"Didn't seem prepared"

"Didn't turn up" arrive

RIGHT
Ensure that you know how to get to the firm, and check the times of buses and trains.
Allow plenty of time to get ready and make whot sure you wear something appropriate. For jobs where you will have a lot of contact with the public, it is obviously particularly important to look smart.
Even if you are nervous, try and seem enthusiastic. Answer questions with more than Yes or No and make sure that you would have some questions ready that you would like to ask.
Find out as much as you can about the job and the company so that you sound interested and informed. Make sure you are ready to answer questions the a list have had u employer may have on his/her checklist.
If you cannot make the appointment for any reason ensure you ring up and explain and, if possible, arrange an alternative date and time.

Turn over for Activities

Interviewer's checklist

☐ Reasons for applying

☐3 Educational background, including exams *5 languages taxi fitst*

☐5 Work experience *sports football*

☐6 Interests and hobbies

☐2 Personal and family background *eyes Barker*

☐4 Health and fitness

Attitudes to:

☐7 carrying weapons

☐8 violence — *not necessary*

☐ crime and punishment

☐9 role of the police *coal for desire*

10 hour
social work
long — sighted
short —

APPLICATION FOR EMPLOYMENT

Surname	Education and examinations
First name(s)	
Address	
Telephone number	
Date of birth	Previous employment
Place of birth	*Social*
Nationality	
Married/single	
Number of children under 18	
Height	Leisure interests
Weight	
Position for which you are applying	
Medical history *anything stop you to work* Give details of any permanent disability, major illnesses, operations, or other health problems which might affect your work.	
	Applicant's signature
	Date

ACTIVITIES

A Choosing a career

1 Your likes, dislikes, abilities and talents will normally mean there is no one but a range of jobs suitable for you. Which of the categories on page 19 best describes your interests?

2 When you have picked the category which best suits you, look through the list of careers and tick the ones which are related to your chosen category. Then show the list to a friend, and see if he/she agrees that these careers would suit you.

3 **Pair work** Of the careers you have ticked, underline the one you would most like to do. Without mentioning its name, describe the job to the person sitting next to you. See if he or she can guess what the job is and what category it belongs to. Does he/she think it would suit you?

4 Group discussion   Choose five of the jobs from the list and grade them according to pay, working conditions, qualifications needed, promotion prospects and job satisfaction. See if you can agree to an order for your chosen jobs, from the least attractive to the most attractive.

5 Game – What's my line? One person chooses a job from the list on page 19. The others must find out what the job is by asking not more than twenty questions which can be answered 'yes' or 'no'.

B   The interview

1 Read through these pieces of advice that might be given to applicants about to go to their first job interviews.

☐ Answer questions as briefly as possible.
☐ Ask questions about the company and job.
☐ Wear clothes suitable for the job.
☐ Take a checklist with you so that you remember what to say.
☐ Never cancel your interview appointment.

☐ Get to the interview on time.
☐ Smile a lot.
☐ Speak slowly and clearly.
☐ Try to control and direct the interview yourself.

Read the texts about interviews on page 19 and tick in the boxes above those pieces of advice which are actually given in the texts.

2 Find words in the texts that mean the same as the words in italics.
a Don't be *untidy*.
b Taking an examination is always very *worrying*.
c *Remember* that an interview is a two-way process. *(three words)*
d You will have a better chance if you appear *keen* and *knowledgeable*.

3 Discussion   Do you agree with the advice given in the texts? Can you think of any more advice to give to a job applicant?

C   Listening comprehension

1 Read the interviewer's checklist and application form on page 20. Then listen to the interview once, and put numbers by the items in the checklist to show the order in which the interviewer asks questions. The first one has been done for you.

2 Listen again and fill in as much as possible of the application form.

3 Compare what happened in this interview with the advice given on page 19. Discuss whether or not this candidate would be suitable for the job.

D   Role play

In pairs, act out an interview between an employer and a job applicant.

1 Together, choose a job and draw up a suitable application form based on the one on page 20. Some of the questions there may not be relevant, and you may think of others that should be included.
2 The applicant should fill in the form, while the employer draws up a checklist of questions and topics.
3 The employer should study the completed application form, and call in the applicant for the interview. Then act out the interview.

COUNTRIES AND COUNTRYSIDE

LANGUAGE STUDY

Vocabulary

Word families:
country, countryside

A Match the definitions and examples.

Examples

a He bought a small plot of *land* to build a house on.
b It's good to get your feet on dry *land* after a long sea voyage.
c *Nature* is often very cruel. *what is around*
d The house is situated in pleasant *surroundings*.
e The *scenery* in Norway was magnificent.
f The Sussex *countryside* is green and rich.
g We spent a day in the *country*.
h How many foreign *countries* have you been to?

Definitions   *Example*

d **1** area near or round a place   ☐
g **2** ground or earth owned as property   ☐
f **3** hills, trees, fields, etc. considered as physical objects ☐
e **4** hills, trees, fields, etc. considered as things to look at ☐
b **5** opposite of sea   ☐
g **6** opposite of town   ☐
c **7** the world and its animals, insects and plants   ☐
h **8** nation or state   ☐

nice adjective
↑
scenery

B Choose the correct word to put in each space.

1 Luckily I have both a flat in the city and a cottage in the _contry_ .
2 She has bought a huge piece of _land_ to build her house on.
3 English is spoken in many _countries_ all over the world.
4 Farming is difficult here because the _land_ is very poor.
5 There's no point in fighting the forces of _nature_ .
6 The _scenery_ in the North of England is very beautiful.
7 After six days of huge waves and heavy rain, we finally sighted _of sea_ . _sea_
8 I'm planning a month's walk through the Scottish _consi dired_
9 A child's development is dependent on the _surrounding_ he is brought up in.
10 I'll always be a _contry_ person. I can't stand the noise and smell of the city.

Now write seven sentences of your own, one for each of the words in italics in the *Examples*.

C Describe the house in the photograph, using as many as possible of the above seven words.

D Word associations

Find words from this list to fill the gaps, and explain the associations.

bank, geography, pass, peak, rock, stream, valley, wood

For example:
boy/girl – man/_____
Answer: *As boy is to girl, so man is to woman.*
Explanation: Boys and girls are male and female children; men and women are male and female adults.

white/black – fat/_____
Answer: *As white is to black, so fat is to thin.*
Explanation: White and black are opposites; so are fat and thin.

1 sea/coast – river/_bank_   5 sea/water – mountain/_rock_
2 kings/history – rivers/_Geography_   6 ocean/sea – river/_stream_
3 mountain/hill – forest/_wood_   7 person/head – mountain/_peak_
4 river/bridge – mountain/_pass_   8 up/down – hill/_valley_

Phrasal verbs: *make*

E Read the sentences and complete the definitions below, by finding expressions from the list in the box which mean the same as the phrasal verbs in italics. Then say the sentences aloud, substituting the correct forms of the alternative expressions.

1 From the summit, I could just *make out* the village on the horizon.
2 The beautiful scenery of the north *made up for* the days we had spent in the flat industrial south.
3 The countryside around us *is made up of* small farms with lakes in between.
4 The foxes *made off* with five lambs in one night.
5 If you don't know the answer, *make up* a suitable one.
6 The journalist *made out* that he was a wealthy landowner.

compensate for	=	_____
consist of	=	_____
invent	=	_____
pretend	=	_____
run away	=	_____
see	=	_____

Write six sentences of your own, each containing one of the phrasal verbs.

Verb review: the past simple and past continuous

Formation of regular verbs: *wait*

Complete the gaps in the tables below.

Past simple		
+	**–**	**?**
I waited.	She _didn't wait_	Did she wait?
We waited.	You did not wait.	_Did_ you wait?
Contractions:		
	I _didn't_ wait.	
	They _didn't_ wait.	

Past continuous		
+	**–**	**?**
I _am waiting_	I was not waiting.	_where_ she waiting?
We were waiting.	We _were_ waiting.	Were they waiting?
Contractions:		
	She wasn't waiting.	_____ she waiting?
	They weren't waiting.	_____ they waiting?

Formation of irregular verbs

A   Make simple questions and answers in the past simple tense.
Examples:

go/Paris/Rome
Did you go to Paris? – No, I didn't go to Paris. I went to Rome.

see/Peter/John
Did you see Peter? – No, I didn't see Peter. I saw John.

1 teach/physics/chemistry
2 leave/at 6 o'clock/at 6.30
3 buy/any oranges/some apples
4 know/Murphy/his wife
5 do/the washing-up/the cleaning
6 have/a nice time/a terrible time
7 speak/to the manager/to the assistant
8 give/her a plant/her some roses
9 get up/early/very late
10 tell/the truth/a lie
   told

Questions in the past simple

B   Think of as many questions as you can to which the information in the sentence below could be the answer. For example, the questions could start with: *Who . . ?, When . .?, Where . .?, What . .?, How much . .?, What sort . .?*

On July 1st 1985, Michael dropped a gold ring worth £500 down a deep hole at the bottom of the garden.

Use of the past simple and past continuous

C   Match up the rules with the examples in italics by writing one letter in each box.

Rules

The **past simple** is used for:
a a single action completed at a definite time in the past
b a repeated action or habit completed within a definite period in the past
c a state completed within a definite period in the past
(N.B. **b** and **c** can also be expressed with *used to*)

The **past continuous** is used for:
d a past action that started before a given time and continued after it
e a past action that started before another action and continued after it
f a past state, particularly in descriptions, that sets the scene when the narrative is in the past simple.
(N.B. The verbs that are not normally used in the present continuous tense – see page 13 – are rarely used in the past continuous tense.)

Example sentences   *Rule*

1 It *rained* three times last week. ☐
2 It *was raining* at six o'clock this morning. ☐
3 It *was getting* dark; I shivered and hurried on. ☐
4 The sun *didn't shine* at all during the whole of January. ☐
5 I *was just leaving* the house when it started to snow. ☐
6 Suddenly lightning *struck* the church tower. ☐
7 I *lived* in the south of England until I was ten years old. ☐
8 While we *were waiting* for the storm to pass, we ate breakfast. ☐
9 At that time I *went* up into the mountains as often as I could. ☐
10 The sun *was rising*; the birds were singing; I felt wonderful. ☐

Contrasting the past simple and past continuous

D   The people in the pictures were staying at a hotel which caught fire when it was suddenly struck by lightning. Ask and answer questions, like this:

What was the man in Room 1 doing when lightning struck? – He was sleeping.
And what did he do when the hotel caught fire? – He shouted 'Help!'

E   Make complete sentences using the past simple and past continuous tenses. For example:

Why/you/not/answer/when/I/ring? – Because/I/have/a bath.
Why didn't you answer when I rang? – Because I was having a bath.

1 I/not/stay/long/ because/they/have/dinner
2 When/I/arrived/ they/still/prepare/the meal
3 I/sleep/soundly/when/a loud noise/wake/me/up
4 I/know/that/something/be/wrong/with/my car/because/water/pour/ from it
5 What/go/on/at your house/when/I/telephone/you?
6 I/hear/the cheers/from the stadium. What/they/applaud?
7 You/watch/the News/last night? – No,/I/still/work/at 9 o'clock
8 The prisoner/escaped/while/the guards/have/their tea–break
9 It/snow/heavily/when/we/get/up/but/it/stop/before/we/leave/the hotel
10 It/not/take/long – by six o'clock/we/chat/like old friends

Grammar revision:
used to, usually, be used to, get used to

A   Match sentences 1–4 to the explanations a–d.

1 He *got used to* driving to work. ☐
2 He *usually* drove to work. ☐
3 He *used to* drive to work. ☐
4 He *was used to* driving to work. ☐

a He didn't mind driving to work. It didn't worry him at all.
b It was his custom to drive to work, but he doesn't drive to work now.
c On most occasions he drove to work, but he sometimes went by train.
d Over a period of time he adjusted, until his dislike of driving to work disappeared.

Definitions: Put the correct expressions in the gaps.

_____ emphasises the habitual or repeated nature of actions and states completed within a definite period in the past.
_____ means the same as *nearly always*, and is used in the present, the future, and the past.
_____ means *be accustomed to*.
_____ means *become accustomed to*.

B   Mr and Mrs Potter and their children used to live in the country. They used to spend a lot of time out-of-doors, and at the weekends they usually went for long walks. Now they live in town. They're getting used to the crowds, but they aren't used to the noise yet.

Look at the pictures opposite and make up more sentences about the Potters using *be used to*, *get used to*, *usually* and *used to*.

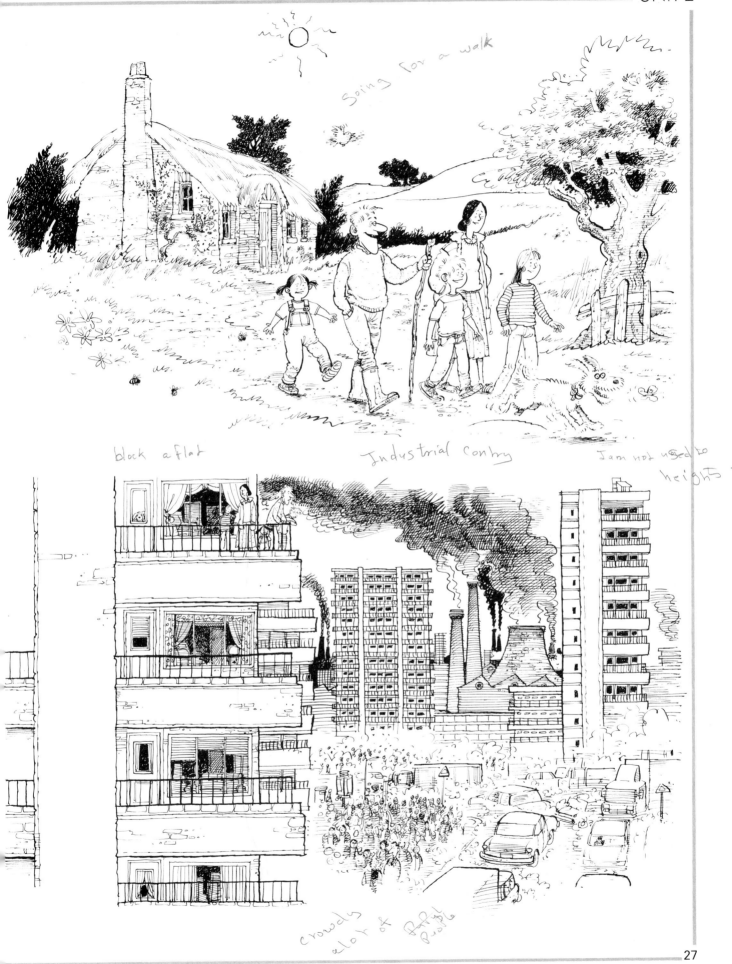

Speech work: sentence stress

In English sentences, some words are stressed while others are unstressed.

Content words (words that carry information) are usually stressed and lengthened	Form words (with a mainly grammatical function) are usually unstressed and shortened
nouns: *country, weather, etc.* adjectives: *beautiful, awful, etc.* adverbs: *only, usually, etc.* demonstratives: *this, that, etc.* verbs (not auxiliaries): *go, etc* interrogative pronouns: *when, etc.*	prepositions: *to, on, etc.* pronouns: *she, me, etc.* conjunctions: *and, if, but, etc.* articles: *a, the, some* auxiliaries: *have, can, etc.* relative pronouns: *who, which, etc.*

Using the table above, say why each of the words in this sentence is stressed or unstressed.

Excuse me, I *won*der if you could *tell* me *where* I can *find books* on the *his*tory of *Swe*den. ~~information~~

One syllable in the sentence is stressed more heavily than any other. This is called the *main stress*, and it is typically placed on the last stressed syllable of the sentence.

Where are the *books* on the *his*tory of *Swe*den?

Main stress can be placed on *any* syllable to show emphasis in meaning.

Respond to each of these statements with the same question as in the example, but changing the main stress each time as appropriate.

We have lots of books on the geography of Sweden.
Yes, but where are the books on the __his__tory of Sweden?

1 We have lots of videos on the history of Sweden.
2 We have lots of books on the history of Norway.
3 Our books on the history of Sweden are very interesting.

Yes but where are they books

Now mark the stressed syllables in the dialogue below and read it aloud.

Yes but where are they videos on the history
books

Functions: asking for and giving information

At the library: a customer and two librarians

Customer Excuse me, I wonder if you could tell me where I can find books about the history of Sweden.

1st lib. I'm afraid I don't know. I'm new here. But my colleague will be able to help you.

2nd lib. Yes, certainly. Go along the corridor and through the first door on your right.

Customer Thank you very much.

2nd lib. Not at all.

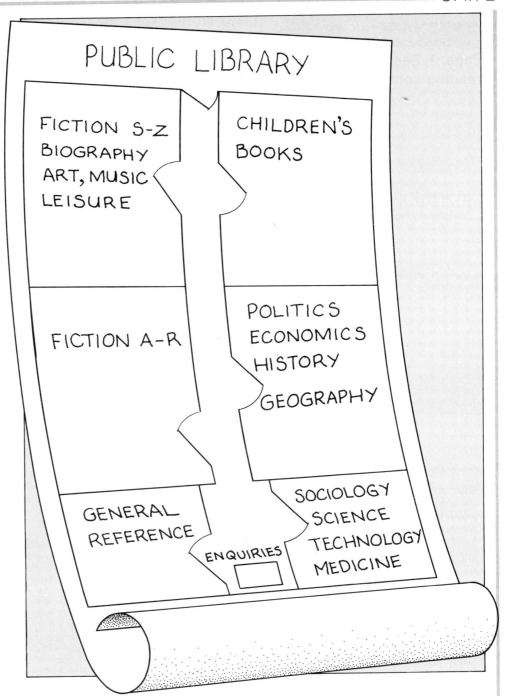

PUBLIC LIBRARY

FICTION S-Z
BIOGRAPHY
ART, MUSIC
LEISURE

CHILDREN'S
BOOKS

FICTION A-R

POLITICS
ECONOMICS
HISTORY
GEOGRAPHY

GENERAL
REFERENCE

ENQUIRIES

SOCIOLOGY
SCIENCE
TECHNOLOGY
MEDICINE

A In groups of three, work out which phrases in the dialogue could be replaced by the following phrases. Then practise reading the dialogue aloud, using the alternatives. Think carefully about stress and rhythm.

Do you know . . .
Yes, of course.
I'm sorry. I can't help you.

Excuse Can you tell me . . .
Don't mention it.
You're welcome.

B Take the parts of customer and librarian talking about where books of various kinds can be found. Use the plan of the library to help you.

EXAM FOCUS

Paper 1, Section B: reading comprehension

This part of the paper consists of three passages, each followed by a number of multiple-choice questions (usually five per passage). Some questions test comprehension of specific points of information; others test a more general understanding of the passage as a whole. One mark is given for each correct answer, with a total of fifteen marks for the section.

First passage: usually a literary text, e.g. from a novel or biography
Second passage: a factual text, e.g. describing a manufacturing process
Third passage: one or more 'practical' texts, e.g. instructions, notices

Dos and don'ts

- Read the instructions. The answers must be written on a separate answer sheet.
- Do one passage at a time. Read passage 1 and answer all of its questions before looking at passage 2.
- Read the whole passage first. Never answer a question until you have read the whole of the relevant passage.
- Allow plenty of time. Give yourself the same amount of time (at least ten minutes) for each passage.
- Mark one answer per question. If you write more than one answer for a question, you will be given no marks.
- Don't be misled. Watch out for words from the passage used in *incorrect* alternatives, or phrases of similar appearances but very different meaning.
- Look at similar alternatives. If two alternatives are very similar, the correct answer will often – but not always – be one of them.
- Check your answers. Make sure your answers reflect the points made in the passage.

Read the text *1066 AD – The Norman Invasion.* Then read both questions. Choose one answer for each question. If you cannot answer them immediately, study the passage again until you can.

1066 AD – The Norman Invasion

Harold the King was waiting in the South for the attack of William of Normandy when he heard that Hardraada had landed in the north and was destroying the countryside. Harold dashed northwards. He gathered as many soldiers as he could on the way and defeated Hardraada in a fierce battle at Stamford Bridge, near York.

But just as he was celebrating the victory, news came that William had landed at Pevensey Bay. South again raced Harold with his soldiers. In less than two weeks he was facing the Norman enemy on the hill of Senlac, a few miles inland from Hastings.

The battle swung first this way, then that. Despite their tiredness after such a long march, the English had the initial advantage, since they were fighting for their country and for their independence. But, in the end, the Normans' discipline won the day, and Harold himself fell when an arrow struck him in the eye.

In this manner the last of the old English kings died, and a new age began.

1 When Hardraada landed, Harold
  A waited in the south.
  B attacked William of Normandy.
  C destroyed the countryside.
  D dashed northwards.

2 The Normans won because
  A Harold was struck in the eye.
  B the English were tired.
  C the Normans were better disciplined.
  D Harold was old.

Now see if you have chosen the correct answers.

1 A is wrong. The passage states that Harold *was waiting* in the south when Hardraada landed. This is not at all the same as *he waited*.
  B is wrong. Harold thought that *William* would attack. The battle between Harold and William took place later.
  C is wrong. Hardraada, not Harold, was destroying the countryside.
  D is right.

2 A is wrong. It is given as a fact, but not as a reason for victory.
  B is wrong. This also is given as a fact, but not as a reason for victory: the English had the initial advantage *even though* they were tired.
  C is *right*. The phrase *the Normans' discipline won the day* means that their discipline was the main cause of victory.
  D is wrong. The phrase *the last of the old English kings* does not mean that Harold was old, but that he was king of 'old England'.

Now answer the following questions, explaining why each of the alternatives is right or wrong.

3 The troops that fought for Harold at Stamford Bridge
   A joined him in the South.
   B joined him during his journey from the South.
   C joined him in the North.
   D joined him during his journey from the North.

4 The battle at Senlac took place almost two weeks after Harold
   A heard that Hardraada had landed.
   B reached York.
   C heard that William had landed.
   D faced the Norman enemy.

5 The new age began because
   A after 1066, all the kings of England were young.
   B after 1066, the kings of England were not English.
   C an arrow struck Harold in the eye.
   D the English became independent.

Composition: narratives (1)

Dos and don'ts

- Write in the past tenses. Use the past simple, past continuous and past perfect for telling a story.
- Don't use the present tenses. Present and future tenses may of course be used in direct speech, but avoid them in the actual narrative.
- Vary action with description. Let the reader relax sometimes; slow down the action by providing background descriptions.
- Vary short and long sentences. Use short sentences to create tension, drama and excitement, longer sentences for more relaxed or descriptive passages
- Plan carefully. Planning a narrative is dealt with more thoroughly in the next unit (page 41).

A   Here is part of the story of the Norman Invasion, with all the rules broken. The conjunctions have been removed to make every sentence short, and the tenses have all been changed to the present. Without referring to the original, rewrite the passage so that it follows the advice given above. Put all the verbs into the past tenses, and join some of the sentences together with suitable conjunctions. You may change the order of the sentences if you wish. Some sentences should be kept short – these will be the sentences where you want to create drama and excitement.

Harold the king waits in the South for the attack of William of Normandy. Hardraada lands in the North. Hardraada destroys the countryside. Harold hears about it. Harold dashes northwards. He gathers as many soldiers as he can on the way. He defeats Hardraada in a fierce battle at Stamford Bridge, near York.

He celebrates the victory. William lands at Pevensey Bay. The news comes. Harold races south again with his soldiers. In less than two weeks he is facing the Norman enemy on the hill of Senlac. Senlac is a few miles inland from Hastings.

B   Make up a story in pairs or small groups, with each student in turn adding a new sentence. Use alternate sentence types like this:

   Student 1: a long descriptive sentence with at least two parts joined by a conjunction
   Student 2: a short dramatic sentence
   Student 3: a long descriptive sentence
   Student 4: a short dramatic sentence

Facts about Britain

wonderfull

absouly correct

Round 1, subject [blank box]

		Score	
		Jenny	Peter
When was the battle of Hastings?		1066	
Which English king broke with the Roman Catholic Church? ?	Henry VIII		
How many wife did henry have ?	Six		
Which Roman general invaded England in 55 BC?	Julien Sucies		
which famous English which ?	Shakespeare 1564		
when the first world did ?	1918		
When were England and Scotland first joined under one king?	1603 william Jan		
which queen and for the time British longest ?	Victoria	19 1 18 17	
		Totals	

Round 2, subject [blank box]

			Score	
			Jenny	Peter
Which is the longest river in Britain?		Severn 7 220 miles		
which is hihest main rain in Britain ?	Ben Nevis Scotland			
Name two of the seas or oceans around Britain.	alantic North sea ocean			
How many city in England have it ?	hire Sea 190 0 Tnhatuston			
Name the capital cities of the four countries in the UK.	Three Birthnishan			
Name two of London's main airports.	Eden Brae Eoxden London			
what the home mountain rain east Ing of the	Heorow Hatini Galwie The Pennines			
which is largest lake rain in England ?	Windermere			
			Totals	

Final score

Jenny 190   Peter 50

The Norman Invasion

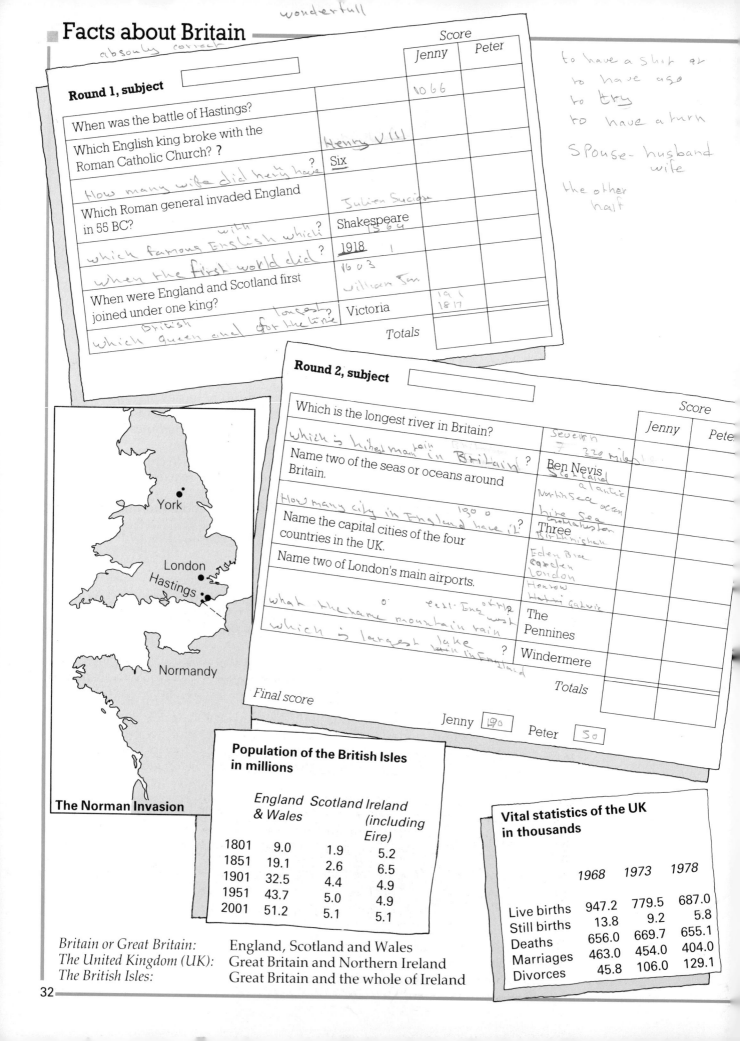

York
London
Hastings
Normandy

Population of the British Isles in millions

	England & Wales	Scotland	Ireland (including Eire)
1801	9.0	1.9	5.2
1851	19.1	2.6	6.5
1901	32.5	4.4	4.9
1951	43.7	5.0	4.9
2001	51.2	5.1	5.1

Vital statistics of the UK in thousands

	1968	1973	1978
Live births	947.2	779.5	687.0
Still births	13.8	9.2	5.8
Deaths	656.0	669.7	655.1
Marriages	463.0	454.0	404.0
Divorces	45.8	106.0	129.1

Britain or Great Britain: England, Scotland and Wales
The United Kingdom (UK): Great Britain and Northern Ireland
The British Isles: Great Britain and the whole of Ireland

ACTIVITIES

A Facts about Britain: a radio quiz show

Listen to the recording of the radio quiz show *Facts about Britain* as many times as you need to. While you are listening, fill in the missing questions and answers on the score sheets opposite, and write down the number of points scored by the contestants for each question.

B Facts about your country

Make up questions about the history and geography of *your* country and hold a radio quiz show. You will need:

● a radio producer, who will make out a timetable for when the recording is to start and end, and will make all the necessary arrangements for the recording.
● a 'quizmaster' to introduce the programme, ask the questions and keep the score
● two teams of contestants

C The Norman invasion

1 Read again the text on page 30 about the Norman invasion.

2 Complete the map on the opposite page by writing in the names of the three places marked with small dots.

3 Look at the map and describe in your own words the events of 1066.

4 Write the story of an important event in the history of *your* country.

D Statistics

1 Discuss the information in the tables opposite. What changes took place over the years? What reasons can you think of for the changes?

2 Imagine that you are writing in the year 2000. Write a brief report on population changes in the British Isles since 1801.

E Describing your country

In groups, make a list of headings under which you could describe your own country. Each student should take one of the headings, and give a short talk on it (after about one minute's preparation).

Geography puzzle

1 Find the words that are defined below and put them in the right order, so that their third letters make a new word that's down even when it's up in the hills!

   a curved part of the coastline (3 letters)
   b land surrounded by water (6)
   c mountain created by explosions in the earth's interior (7)
   d situation or surroundings in which we live (11)
   e top of mountain (4)
   f very large amount of salt water (5)

2 Make up a puzzle of your own. Find a five-letter word in one of the exercises in this unit. Then find five other words whose first letters make up that word. Write definitions for these words and give the definitions to another group of students to solve.

UNIT 3 A PLACE TO LIVE

Vocabulary

(handwritten annotations on pictures:)
- block of flat
- thatched / grass / cottage
- mansion
- bungalow
- semi-detached
- villa
- Pamtree / thatnice / Building
- Terraced house

Word families:	flat	bungalow	block of flats
houses and homes	house	villa	building
	cottage	mansion	home

A Choose one word from the list above to describe each of the pictures

B Which of the nouns on page 34 could these words go with? Some may go with more than one.

single-storey _building_
high-rise _block flat_
family _house_ , *home, cottage, flat*
suburban _house, flat, mansion_
country _villa, house, mansion_
picturesque _cottage, house, bungalow_
luxurious _mansion, house, a_ *expensive*

historical cottage
oldg-worldy

holiday _Flat, bungalow, house_
retirement _bungalow, flat_
historic _building_ , *semi detached, cottage*
detached _house, cottage, bungalow_
semi-detached _house_
terraced _house, cottage_

C Discuss the advantages of each kind of accommodation. Which would you like to live in and where would it be? What are the reasons for your choice?

Phrasal verbs: *run*

D Match the definitions with the phrasal verbs in sentences 1–8.

a allow to increase
b have no more supplies
c meet by chance
d wear out
e drive a vehicle over
f make quickly
g talk about quickly
h meet (an obstacle)

1 I *ran into* Jack in town yesterday. I hadn't seen him for months.
2 Our cat was killed last week – she was *run over* by a car.
3 It's likely that the world will *run out* of oil within fifty years.
4 They began by *running through* what had been said at the previous meeting.
5 The anti-nuclear campaign has *run up against* a lot of dificulties.
6 Do you like this material? I'm going to *run up* a skirt this afternoon.
7 The twins *ran through* six pairs of shoes in three months.
8 The council has unfortunately *run up* huge debts.

Now make your own sentences, one for each phrasal verb.

Verbs easily confused: *come* and *go*

E Read the dialogue carefully. Then complete the table of definitions, writing the numbers of the examples in the dialogue next to the appropriate definitions. For one of the definitions, both *come* and *go* can be used.

Kim: Are you going (1) to the meeting in London tonight?
Joe: Yes. Do you want to come (2) too? Ann is coming (3) here to pick me up at 7.30. Why don't you come (4) with us? We must stop that factory being built. I may go (5) to the demonstration tomorrow too, if I can persuade someone else to go (6) with me.
Kim: Well, I can't go (7) tonight. But if you want me to go (8) with you tomorrow, I will. I'll come (9) to your house at 9 o'clock.

Definitions	Come/go	Examples
For movement towards the speaker, use	_____	_____
For movement towards the listener, use	_____	_____
For movement away from both the speaker and the listener when the words *with me* or *with us* or *with you* are stated or implied, use	_____	_____
In all other cases, use	_____	_____

F Write the correct forms of *come* and *go* in the spaces.

I'm _____ away tomorrow for a few days in the country. Why don'
you _____ and join me? I tell you what: rather than _____ on
your own, you could _____ here first, or perhaps you'd prefer
Mike to _____ and fetch you? Either way, we can _____ down
together and I'm sure we'll have a good time. A friend of mine,
Johnny, will be _____ with us, and a couple of other friends have
already _____ there to get things ready.

Verb review: the present perfect and past perfect

Formation

Complete the gaps in the tables below.

Present perfect simple		
+	**–**	**?**
I _____	They haven't taken.	Have they taken?
He has taken.	He _h_____	_____ he _____?
Present perfect continuous		
I have been taking.	They _have_____	Have they been taking?
He _has_____	It _____	_____ she _____?
Past perfect simple		
I _____	He hadn't taken.	_____ they _____?
Past perfect continuous		
I _____	He _____	_____ they _____?

Use of the present perfect

A Read the examples and tick the correct boxes to show the difference
in use between the **present perfect** and **past simple** tenses.

I have been to many places in my life.
I went to lots of places in 1970.
I haven't talked to John this week.
I didn't talk to him last week either.

Which tense is used for . . .?	Present perfect	Past simple
time periods stretching from the past up to the present		
time periods completed in the past		

B Put the verbs into the correct tenses, present perfect or past simple.

1 I _moved_ (move) to this house six years ago.
2 I _have_____ (live) here for six years.
3 The council _decided_ (decide) to renovate a lot of old houses.
4 The council _builde_ (build) a lot of flats in the 1970s.
5 Sir Christopher Wren _____ (design) St. Paul's Cathedral.
6 This is the first time he _has_____ (own) a house.

Use of the past perfect

The **past perfect** is used to talk about something that happened before a
certain point in the past. For example:

When he arrived he told us about all the countries he had been to (i.e. before he
arrived).

C   Put the verbs into the past simple or the past perfect tense.

1 I __had__ (visit) him on March 1st. I __had__ ~~met~~ (meet) him only once before.
2 When he __became__ (come) back, I __had__ (just finish) the job.
3 I __thought__ (think) that I __had known~~kne~~__ (know) her face, but I couldn't remember where I __'seen__ (see) her.
4 Clearly he __had__ (read) the book several times, because he __knew__ (know) everything about it.   __taken__
5 When they __have~~got~~__ (get) there, someone __had__ (already take) the room.

Both the present perfect and past perfect tenses are often used with such words as: *never, ever, just, already, yet, for, since*. Examples:

> I've *never* been to China.
> When they got married, they had *never* met before.

Write your own sentences using each of the words in the above list with each tense.

The **present perfect continuous** is used for an action that started in the past and continues up to (or beyond) the present. The **past perfect continuous** is used for an action that started before a given point in the past and continued up to (or beyond) that point. For example:

> *I have been looking for a house for a year* (and I still am).
> *When I found my flat, I had been looking for two years* (right up to the time I found it).

In 1985 this house was for sale. It was in a terrible state. An old lady had been living in it for fifty years and in that time she hadn't done anything to it.

Bob and Sue bought the house and since 1985 it has changed completely. They have spent a lot of money and modernised the house completely.

D 1 Look at the first picture and then make sentences from these cues
to describe what had or hadn't happened by 1985.
  a Vandals/break/windows *had been breaking*
  b Old lady/live/no bathroom/50 years *had been living*
  c No one/paint/since/built *had Painting*
  d Neighbours/complain/the Council/months *had complained to*
  e House/become/damp *had become*

2 Look at the second picture and then make sentences to describe
what has or hasn't happened up to now.
  a They/live/there/1985 *haven't Pre time 1989*
  b They/take down/old toilet *had Pre*
  c They/paint/whole house
  d They/work/very hard/since 1985
  e They/not/finish/yet

3 Discuss why you think the house was for sale in 1985. What do
you think had happened in the old lady's life?
4 What else do you think Bob and Sue have done to this house?
5 Why do you think they bought this house. What had happened in
their lives before that?

Here are some words to use in your answers if you like:

old people's home   ill   *had just* just married   kitchen
hospital   save money   <u>afford</u>   central heating
bathroom   died   sold flat   *have Putting*

Grammar revision: *to get/have something done*

Formation

A Fill in the table with words from this list, adjusting the verb forms
where necessary.

the house, wash, my photograph, paint, cut down

	get/have	object	past participle
I must	have / get	the car *washed*	
I	had / got *my*	*Photograph*	taken
She'll	have / get	*cut* the tree	
I'd like to	have / get	*the house Painting*	

Meaning

To get something done means to make arrangements for someone else to
do a job on one's behalf, often for money.

B Look at this picture of some
disused land. Two officials are
talking about making it into a
children's play area. At the moment
it is full of rubbish, the grass is very
long, the fence is broken, the
surface is full of holes, and there are
<u>weeds</u> growing.

kind of grass

land
waste land   derelict land
disused land

Of course, these men will not do any of the work themselves, so use these cues to make sentences they may say. For example:

First/must/rubbish/take away
First, we must get the rubbish taken away.

1 Then/should/fence/mend   Then
2 After that/must/weeds/kill
3 Next/need to/grass/cut   Next must need to cut the grass
                                                    have to
4 Finally/have to/area/resurface   The man have to finally clean the area
                                                                                the surface

Now make more sentences of your own to suggest what they will get done after that. Think about swings, slides, a football pitch, and so on.

to erect   put up   cut down
            lay

Speech work: falling intonation

Falling intonation is the pattern normally used for:
a statements of fact
b questions beginning with a question word like *Who, Where, How, Why.*

The voice starts to fall on the last main stressed syllable of the sentence and continues to fall until the end of the sentence.

I'm feeling ⟶ *terrible.*
Why did you ⟶ *hit him?*

A Mark the last main stress in these sentences and read them aloud.

1 What have they decided to do about the land?
2 How much is it going to cost?
3 Where is the money coming from?
4 Why do they want to do it?
5 Who will benefit from it?

B In pairs, ask and answer the questions in A about the piece of wasteland in the picture on page 39.

C Now mark the intonation on the last main stress of each sentence in Joan and Bill's dialogue below. Then practise reading it aloud.

Functions: expressing likes, approval and preferences

Joan: What do you think of the plans for the new children's playground?
Bill: I was very impressed. I think they have designed it well. What about you?
Joan: I certainly prefer it to the original idea of using the space for tennis courts. We've got enough of those already.
Bill: So do I. I think they've got their priorities right at last.

A Which phrases in the dialogue could be replaced by the expressions listed below? Practise reading the dialogue aloud using alternative expressions where possible.

Alternative expressions
I think it's wonderful/delightful/
   delicious, etc.
I'm very keen on . . .
I thought it was very well done.
It is well worth doing/seeing.
How do you feel about . . .?
It's great/awful.
It's much better/worse (than . . .)
I like . . . more (than . . .)

B In pairs, hold similar conversations about the following. Use the alternative expressions listed above whenever you can.

1 A restaurant has just opened.
2 A new building has been built in the middle of an old village.
3 A proposal has been made to ban heavy traffic from the centre of a small town.

EXAM FOCUS

Paper 3, Section A: gap filling

Dos and don'ts

This question consists of a passage with twenty gaps in it. You have to fill each gap with *one* word only. The missing word may be *any* type of word – article, preposition, noun, verb, etc.

● Read through the whole passage first.
● Don't write in any words until you have read it all.
● Make sure you have understood the general sense.
● Ask yourself:
  when and where the passage is set
  whether the time changes
  what happens
  what the connection is between the points.
● Write in the words that are obvious to you first. Then go back and do the more difficult ones.
● If a word is difficult, decide first what kind of word it must be e.g. a preposition, article, verb, noun, etc.
● Make sure you write something in every space, even if you don't know what the correct word is – have a try.

A   Read through this passage. Before filling in the gaps, answer questions 1–5.

On the wall in my bedroom there _____ (1) a photograph _____ (2) my grandfather. My grandfather died a long time _____ (3) and his picture often _____ (4) me of my childhood when I _____ (5) to go fishing and hunting _____ (6) him.
    Recently, I _____ (7) his old hunting jacket _____ (8) of the cupboard and for some _____ (9) held it _____ (10) my face. Suddenly I _____ (11) a child again. I _____ (12) feel his cheek against mine and _____ (13) his voice. _____ (14) a moment I was _____ (15) my grandfather's house again listening to _____ (16) about his youth. They _____ (17) all there – his age, his tobacco, _____ (18) life – in the smell _____ (19) that old _____ (20).

1 Is the passage about the past, present or future?
2 Where does the time change?
3 What places are mentioned?
4 Does the writer go to his grandfather's house?
5 Why does he start thinking about his grandfather?

Now fill in the gaps in the way suggested above.

B   In pairs, choose a passage from a newspaper or book. Write out the passage with some of the words missing. Make sure the words you take out can be guessed from the meaning of the text.
Exchange exercises with another pair and fill in the gaps made by the other pair.
(Don't forget that in some cases there could be more than one correct answer.)

Composition: narratives (2)

Dos and don'ts

● It is very important to plan your story before you begin to write.
● Don't make up the story as you go along.
● Decide on the order in which you are going to describe the events.
● Decide how much is going to be in each paragraph.
● Don't write fewer than 120 words – you will lose marks.
● Don't write a lot more than 180 words – you will not gain anything and you may lose.

Sequencing

Here are some of the words that can be used for putting ideas in sequence: *after, when, while, then, next, finally, at first, as.*

A Look at the picture story and choose suitable words to put in the spaces.

1 _when_ they were looking in the paper, they noticed a flat.
2 _then at first_ they thought it would be too expensive.
3 _as_ they were walking along the street, they were very impressed.
4 _After_ looking at the outside, they rang the bell.
5 _then_ they went in.
6 _while_ they were looking, they asked a lot of questions.

In some sentences you could use more than one of the words. Which are they?

Now make your own sentences about the events of the rest of the story, using these words.

Paragraphs

Your story should be told in at least three paragraphs:

1 In the first paragraph you should set the scene, describe the place and the people and what they were doing at the beginning of the story.
2 In the middle paragraphs you should tell the main story.
3 In the last paragraph you should say what the result was.

quiet happy

'Flashback' technique

It is not always necessary to start at the beginning of the story. You can make your story more interesting by using the 'flashback' technique. That is, you can begin in the middle or even at the end of the story and then go back to the beginning later on. If you do this you must be very careful about tenses. Look carefully at the tenses in this example:

As Tom and I were walking along the street, we began to feel that we were very lucky to have found this place. We had been looking for a flat for a long time and only the day before we had found this one in the local paper. We had telephoned immediately and made an appointment to see it.

Past Simple
Past Perfect

B Write a narrative based on the picture story.

1 Discuss how many paragraphs the story should have and where the paragraphs should begin and end.
2 Write the story in 120 to 180 words. Write as if you were one of the students. Add extra information about yourself, the flat etc., and a description of the place.
3 Which of the following titles fits the story best? Why?
   a The day a friend narrowly escaped death.
   b Write a story ending with the words 'What a lucky escape!'.
   c The day you saved a life.
   d Living in big cities can be dangerous for young people. Discuss.

C Write plans for all of the following titles. Then write one of the stories in 120 to 180 words.

1 Write a story ending with the words: 'Then I understood why people said the house was haunted.'
2 You were watching television one evening when you saw water running down the hall. Describe what happened next.
3 The busiest day of my life.

DITCHLING

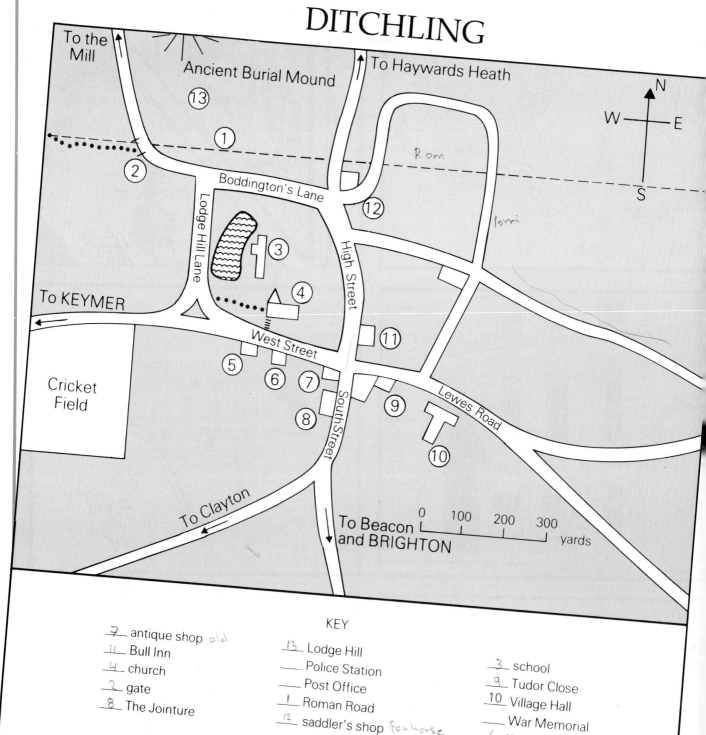

To the Mill

Ancient Burial Mound

⑬

To Haywards Heath

N

W — E

S

① Boddington's Lane

②

Lodge Hill Lane

③

④

To KEYMER

West Street

⑤

⑥

⑦

High Street

⑪

South Street

⑧

⑨

Lewes Road

⑩

Cricket Field

Rom

lom

⑫

To Clayton

To Beacon and BRIGHTON

0   100   200   300
yards

KEY

7 antique shop old	13 Lodge Hill	3 school
11 Bull Inn	___ Police Station	9 Tudor Close
4 church	___ Post Office	10 Village Hall
2 gate	1 Roman Road	___ War Memorial
8 The Jointure	12 saddler's shop For horse	6 White Horse Inn Bull Inn
		5 Wings Place

Proposals to improve the traffic flow in and around Ditchling

Background

×3 times

The volume of traffic has trebled in the last five years. This is due mainly to heavy lorries using the road from Haywards Heath to Clayton as a short cut between London and the South *exhaust* Coast. Many of the historic buildings are showing signs of *lorries* *nogood* decay, brought on by the continuous vibrations and fumes. The *bad* health of the villagers has deteriorated noticeably, with a *lungs* marked increase in bronchial complaints. The number of road accidents has risen sharply, with children on their way to and from school particularly at risk.

A	Proposals	B
To build a by-pass running north from the Clayton Road across the farmland and cricket field as far as the gate on Lodge Hill Lane, then following the course of the Roman road eastwards for 300 yards, and finally turning north to link up with the Haywards Heath road north of the village.		To erect traffic lights at the crossroads; to ban heavy lorries from the village and its approach roads; to mark out pedestrian crossings, particularly on the main routes to the school; to widen part of the High Street (the old saddler's shop will have to be pulled down). *no more*

Handwritten notes (left margin):
1 Her day in the shop normal day routine
2 She ate supper and went to bed
3 The lorry crashed into her house
4 she woke up and stared at the lorry

They fell in love and had breakfast together

A Chance Meeting

happy
Virginia yawned contentedly and switched off the light. Her day in the shop had been quite routine. A few customers had browsed — *having a look* one had even bought something — and at six o'clock she had locked up and gone upstairs to eat supper and retire early to bed.

A long-drawn-out screeching sound woke her, interrupted by a bang that sent glass and bricks flying. Virginia sat up.

Staring at her from the foot of the bed on the first floor of this historic building in the heart of the village was a lorry driver. Virginia knew he was a lorry driver because he was still in his lorry. Incredibly, he seemed unharmed. He even managed a shy smile, and she smiled back.

Later, they ate breakfast together in the hotel opposite. Outside, men and cranes struggled to bring the giant lorry back to earth. It sat up against the wall of the house like a dog begging for biscuits, its head poked inside. No-one ever understood how it had got there. Virginia and the lorry driver, smiling at each other, didn't care.

Turn over for Activities

ACTIVITIES

A   A village walk

1 Listen to the recording from beginning to end without stopping and answer these questions.

   a What is the purpose of the recording?
   b Who has it been made for?
   c Where would you expect to be able to hear of it?

2 Look at the map on page 44 and listen to the recording again. Each time you are told to, stop the tape and write down the numbers of the buildings and other features that have been mentioned. Not everything in the list is mentioned on the tape.

3 Discussion

   a What amenities does Ditchling offer its residents, according to the recording? Would you like to live there?
   b What *other* amenities would you expect a village to provide?
   c Would Ditchling be an interesting place to visit?

B   Role play debate

1 Read the text about Ditchling's traffic problems and the two proposals that have been put forward to solve them. Mark on your maps the route of the proposed by-pass.

2 You are all residents of Ditchling. Divide these roles amongst the class:

Ditchling's oldest resident	doctor	builder
owner of the old saddler's shop	farmer	grocer
manager of The Bull	teacher	policeman
owner of the antique shop	vicar	pupil at the school

Which proposal would you like to support? Individually, make a list of the advantages of your preferred proposal and the disadvantages of the other one.

3 Hold a debate in the village hall. One resident argues briefly in favour of one proposal and against the other. A second resident agrees or disagrees with the first, giving reasons, and adds a further argument. And so on, until everyone has spoken. Finally, take a vote on the proposals.

C   Group work

1 Draw a map of the area where you live or another place that you know well.

2 Mark on it the buildings that would be most interesting to visitors.

3 Write a commentary like the one you have listened to.

D   A Chance Meeting

1 Read the story on page 45 carefully and choose the best answers to these questions.

   a Virginia was contented because _____
     A   it had been an interesting day.
     B   it had been a normal day.
     C   no one had bought anything.
     D   several people had bought things.

   b Virginia probably sold _____ in her shop.
     A   books
     B   food
     C   furniture
     D   kitchen equipment

c When Virginia woke up, she _____
  A screamed.
  B stared at the lorry.
  C stayed in bed.
  D went to the foot of the bed.

d The lorry driver probably came into the bedroom through the
  _____
  A ceiling.
  B door.
  C floor.
  D wall.

e Virginia and the lorry driver _____
  A could see a dog by the house.
  B knew why the lorry had crashed.
  C were glad to meet each other.
  D wondered why the lorry had crashed.

2 Compare the story with the advice about narratives given on pages 41 and 43.

  a **Length**
    Would this story be acceptable in the examination?

  b **Sequencing**
    Which of the words practised in the sequencing exercise are used here to show the order in which events occurred? What other techniques are used to do this?

  c **Flashbacks**
    How does the story use the flashback technique? What changes would have to be made if flashbacks were *not* used? Rewrite as much of the story as necessary in order to avoid flashbacks.

  d **Paragraphs**
    Does the story follow the advice given about paragraphs? Analyse the contents of each paragraph by writing notes containing the key words and ideas, like this:

Paragraph 1	Virginia – Switched off light. Day-routine.
Paragraph 2	She ate
Paragraph 3	
Paragraph 4	The

3 Using your notes as a guide, tell the story in your own words.

4 In 120–180 words, write a story of your own with the title 'A chance meeting'. Spend about five minutes writing a plan containing the key ideas. Then spend a further ten minutes writing the actual story.

A   Choose the best word or phrase to complete each sentence.

1 After I _____ finished working, I switched off the machine.
A have   (B) had   C having   D to have

2 I couldn't find _____ information about the trip.
(A) any   B an   C some   D no

3 He couldn't afford to _____ his car repaired.
A pay   B make   C do   (D) get

4 If you run _____ Steve, give him my best wishes.
A over   B up   (C) into   (D) to

5 My brother lives on the fifteenth floor of that _____ of flats.
(A) block   B building   C tower   D house

6 He went on a long holiday to get _____ his illness.
A through   (B) over   C by   D away

7 They bought the children an ice cream to _____ for their disappointment.
4 happy
(A) compensate   B reconcile   C get over   D make

8 Two _____ were sacked, because they were always turning up late.
A applicants   B applications   (C) employees
D employers

9 Please _____ in mind that your appearance and dress are very important.
(A) bear   B carry   C have   D hold

10 I'm afraid those clothes are not at all _____ for the occasion.
(A) appropriate   B fitted   C matching   D suiting

11 In Norway, I felt inspired by the awesome _____ in the mountains.
A country   B landscape   C nature   (D) scenery

12 Many 18-year-olds are tired of being _____ on their
I am on my parents dependent parents.
A dependant   (B) dependent   C independence
D independent

13 The chapel was built as a _____ to those who died in the war.
in of those who died
(A) memorial   B memory   C remembrance
D souvenir

14 The children can get to school five minutes earlier if they take a short _____ through the vicar's garden.
(A) cut   B link   C pass   D path

15 Unfortunately the library provides no _____ for photocopying.
use for people s thing
A amenities   B chances   (C) facilities
D opportunities

B Put *one* word in each of the numbered spaces.

As I was walking home one summer evening I felt that something
unusual _____ ~~was~~ (1) happening. A small crowd _____ ~~was~~ (2) **had**
gathered by the roadside. I _____ ~~came~~ (3) closer _____ ~~to~~ (4) see
what they were looking _____ ~~at~~ (5). Someone was _____ (6) ~~lying~~
on the pavement. _____ ~~was~~ (7) he dead? _____ ~~had~~ (8) he jumped
_____ ~~and~~ (9) fallen? _____ ~~Did~~ (10) he need help? I asked myself all
~~these~~ this _____ (11) questions _____ ~~and~~ (12) then I _____ ~~concluded~~ (13) that
nobody else seemed worried. (Meanwhile) While (14) I was wondering what to
_____ ~~do~~ (15), it started to rain, just on the spot where the man
_____ (16) lying. He shouted something that I _____ (17) not
hear, but didn't move. It was _____ ~~later~~ (18) that I noticed the film
cameras a few yards in _____ ~~front~~ (19) of me and _____ ~~was~~ (20) a
well known actress who was standing in the shadows. **also**

C Complete the sentences with the appropriate form of either *make* or
do.

Example: *He has just* _____ made _____ *the tea.*

1 I usually have my hair _____ done _____ on Saturday morning.
2 I have never _____ make _____ a mistake like that before.
3 After _____ making my decision, I did not turn back.
4 He was talking so quietly that I couldn't _____ make _____ out what he
was saying.
5 Will somebody please _____ do _____ the washing-up?

D Change the word in capitals to form a word that fits the space.

Example: *Measure the* _____ length _____ *and the width.* *LONG*

1 It is usually forbidden to destroy _historic_ buildings. HISTORY
2 The old couple have saved a lot of money for their
retirement RETIRE
3 The old fishing village is very _Picturesque_ PICTURE
4 _unemploy_ is a serious problem in many countries. EMPLOY
5 The _Industri_ area of the city is not very attractive. INDUSTRY
6 The alpine _landscape_ is very dramatic. LAND
7 Many _homeless_ families have to live in hotels. HOME
8 Have you got any _suggestion_? SUGGEST

E Which sentence in each pair matches the sentence on the right? Give
reasons for your choice.

1 a Have you cut your hair?
  b Have you had your hair cut?

☑ b Has someone else cut your hair?

2 a I've read today's newspaper.
  b I've been reading today's
    newspaper.

☑ a I'll read the rest of it later on.

3 a He wrote a great many
    novels.
  b He has written a great many
    novels.

☑ a And he is planning to write
    another one.

4 a Nobody here smokes.
  b Nobody here is smoking.

☑ a Everybody here is a non-
    smoker.

Handwritten margin notes:
I am not use Dictionnary
sleeping is a good guess!
Good effort - well done

a short time ago

5 a I was just crossing a busy road when I heard the explosion.
b I had just crossed a busy road when I heard the explosion.

☑ I was on the pavement when heard the explosion.

6 a Would you like some cake?
b Would you like a cake?

☑ Let me cut a piece for you.

7 a I need some light.
b I need some lights. *un*

☑ Please draw the curtains.

8 a What have you been doing?
b What have you done?

b ☑ What have you finished doing?

F Put the verbs in brackets into the correct tenses.

It _had been_ (be) a long day, but by 9 o'clock the children _had gone_ (go) to bed. They _had clear_ (clear) away the supper things and now they _were looking_ (look) forward to a couple of hours in front of the television. Unfortunately the film _was been_ (be) rather boring. Jim soon *fell* _fallen_ (fall) asleep and Sue _started_ (start) to think about all her work. She _was Saw_ (be) sure she _heard_ (hear) a noise outside the window, so she _looked_ (look) up. A shadow _was moving_ __ (move) slowly through the garden. Her heart _raced_ (race). She _turned_ (turn) out the light so that she _couldn't_ (can) see better. There _was_ (be) nobody there. But she _saw_ (see) that it _had been snowing_ (snow) earlier that evening, and across the grass there _was_ (be) a line of footprints. A fox _had walked_ (walk) across right in front of their window, and now it _was looking_ (look) at her from the far corner of the garden.

UNIT 4 TRAVEL

LANGUAGE STUDY
Vocabulary

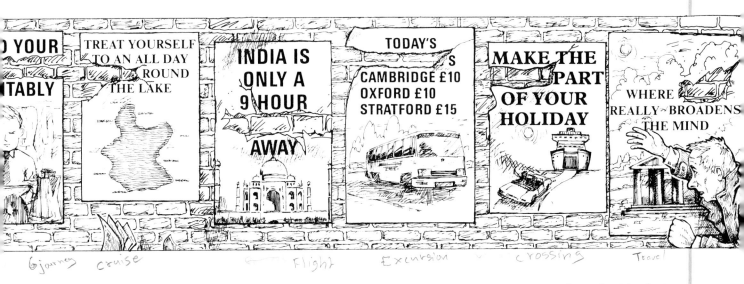

[handwritten annotations on posters: 6journey cruise, Flight, Excursion, Crossing, Travel]

Word families: travel

A   Look at these examples. Then write the correct words in the blanks in the posters above.

1 The train *journey* from Paris to Moscow takes 24 hours.
2 Unfortunately he got seasick during the *voyage* to Australia.
3 How many students are going on the *excursion* to Cambridge?
4 We had a rough *crossing* from Dover to Calais, because there was a storm in the North Sea.
5 Let's go for a *drive* this afternoon. I've just bought a new car.
6 He's been on three business *trips* in the last month – to Paris, Tokyo and Moscow.
7 *Travel* is a waste of time for people who are not able to adapt to new customs and traditions.
8 We have just come back from a *cruise* around the Greek Islands. The boat was like a floating luxury hotel.
9 I would love to experience a *flight* on a plane like Concorde.

Write your own sentences to show the meanings of the words in italics.

Phrasal verbs: *set*

B   Match the expressions with *set* with definitions a–d which follow. Two expressions have the same definition.

1 They *set out* to climb the mountain full of hope, but they came back defeated.
2 The pop group took two hours to *set up* their equipment before the concert.
3 If we are to be at the airport by 8 o'clock, we'll have to *set off* at 6.
4 The bad weather *set* the explorers *back* five days.
5 I was offered a new word processor, but I had no idea how to *set about* using it.

Definitions

a begin a journey, leave <u>Set out</u>
b prevent progress, delay <u>set back</u>
c begin a task <u>Set about</u>
d arrange equipment or furniture for a certain purpose <u>set up</u>

C   Replace the words in italics with phrasal verbs with *set*. One change in word order needs to be made. What is it?

sent

Set off   *Set out*

We *left the house* (1) very early in the morning, because we wanted to get to the camp site and *organise* (2) our equipment before the heat of *Set up* the day. Unfortunately, terrible traffic jams on the motorway *delayed* (3 *Set about* us two hours, and we had to *begin* (4) putting the tent up at two o'clock in the afternoon, before having a well-earned rest.

set back

Verbs easily confused:
bring and *take*

D · Read the conversation, and then complete the definitions with *bring* and *take*.

(On the telephone, the day before leaving for a holiday.)

Mark: Don't forget to *take* something to read on the plane.
Lucy: I think I've read everything I've got. Could you *take* something for me?
Mark: Well, if you like, I'll *bring* a few books round to your house this evening, and you can choose one.
Lucy: Great. Why not *bring* some of your cassettes, too? There are one or two I'd love to *take* with us.
Mark: I'll get Jane to *bring* you some on her way home from work. But you mustn't *take* too many things with you. Remember to leave space in your suitcase for all the souvenirs you'll be *bringing* home

<u>Bring</u> is used for movement towards the place where the speaker is.
<u>Bring</u> is used for movement towards the place where the listener is.
<u>take</u> is used for movement towards places other than those where the listener and speaker are.

E   Put the correct form of *bring* or *take* in the spaces. Make a note of other expressions that are used with *take*.

to take notice of

Dear Janet,
   I am having a wonderful time in India. This really is a relaxing place, I'm glad I <u>took</u> (1) no notice of John's complaints.
   You know you asked me to <u>bring</u> (2) back some local cloth for you? Well, I can't find anything very nice. Mike <u>took</u> (3) me to the market the other day and there was nothing. So, instead I'm <u>bringing</u>(4) you a surprise. I hope you won't be disappointed. There is so much wonderful craft here. I want to <u>bring</u> (5) it all home to England. I would love to <u>take</u> (6) some over to America at Christmas. The only problem is money! I wish I had <u>brought</u>(7) more.
   See you soon. Thanks for <u>taking</u> (8) care of the house for me. I'll <u>take</u> (9) you out to dinner when I get back to England.

                                                                    Love,
worry is not nessasy   Joe

P.S. Don't bother to meet me at the airport. I'll <u>Take</u> (10) a taxi.

Verb review: the future

Set off

Read the dialogue and notice which tenses are used.

Pla

Paul: Hello, Jim. A bit cold, isn't it?

Jim: Yes, and I think *it's going to rain* (1) soon – it's getting darker by the minute. What are you rushing about for?

Paul: *We're going* (2) to the Costa Blanca tomorrow. I've just collected the tickets.

Jim: Lucky you! *Are you flying?* (3)

Paul: Yes. Our plane *takes* (4) off at seven in the morning.

Jim: How on earth *are you going to get* (5) to the airport?

Paul: *We're going to take* (6) the car and leave it in the airport car park.

Jim: I'd get there early, if I were you. The airport *will probably be* (7) very crowded, as it's the high season. I expect *you'll fly* (8) over France, so maybe *you'll see* (9) the forest fires.

Paul: Maybe. I don't know. Anyway, tell Jean that *I'll phone* (10) her at about nine o'clock on Sunday night – and that's a promise! Oh, I've just remembered. I haven't told my boss *we're going* (11) away.

Jim: Oh, don't worry about that. *I'll phone* (12) him in the morning.

A Find examples in the above dialogue of the following uses of the future tenses. Write the numbers of the examples and the actual tenses used (*going to* + infinitive, present continuous, present simple, or *will* + infinitive).

		Examples	Tense
(4) **1** something that is officially timetabled		___	*Present Simple*
10 **2** a promise or threat		___	___
7 **3** a guess about the future, often with expressions such as *I think, I'm sure, probably, surely, perhaps, maybe*		___	*will*
2 **4** a prediction based on something that can be seen now		___	*Pre*
80 **5** an unpremeditated action, one that has not been planned in advance		___	*9*
3 2 **6** a definite arrangement		___	*P. Con*
6 **7** an intention or plan without specific arrangements		___	*Futu*

Notes

● Be careful not to use the *will* future too much. It is safest to restrict it to the three cases described above.

● *Shall* is most commonly used together with *I* and *we* when making:
1 offers, e.g. *Shall I carry the cases?*
2 suggestions, e.g. *Shall we go to France this year?*
3 requests for suggestions, e.g. *What shall I take with me?*

● After *if, unless, when, after, before, until, while, as soon as* when referring to the future, a **present tense** is always used. e.g.
*I'm going to book my holiday as soon as I **know** the dates.* *Present Simple*
*I'll write my postcards while **I'm lying** on the beach.* *P- continous*

● The **perfect tense** is used with a future meaning in sentences like:
*When I **have paid** for my holiday, I'll see how much is left.*

B Now complete the tables of comparatives and superlatives.

1 How ___longer___ will (you) _____ spend the weekend?
   I _____ paint the house. I've just bought the paint.
2 Don't bother your father. I __will__ help you. It's all right. He
   _____ mind.
3 I'm sure they _____ arrive soon.
4 What _____ (you) _____ do with that ladder?
   I _____ climb up on to the roof.
5 Let's watch. That plane _____ take off in a couple of minutes.

C Complete the sentences.

1 Don't unfasten your safety belts until ___the plane has taken off___
2 We'll leave as soon as ___the tube/air___.
3 We won't be able to get there before ___4 o'clock___.
4 After ___having, we Americ the c___ I would like to go to Africa.
5 While ___sight seen in London___, I'll buy some souvenirs.

D Look at this extract from a travel brochure and put the verbs in brackets in the correct tense to comment on and predict what the future holds for the people on this tour. Sometimes more than one tense may be correct. Then describe in your own words what you think will happen on the rest of the tour.

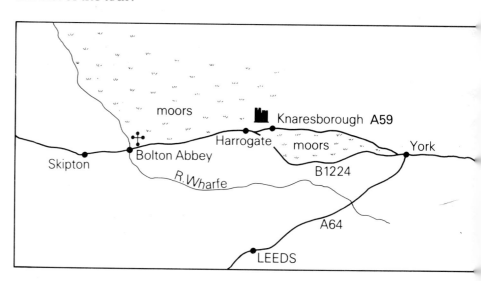

Sunday
Breakfast 8-9am
Departure 9.30am
Depart from Leeds to the cathedral city of York – see the famous railway museum, the Shambles, the Minster, or simply admire the shops. After lunch, a picturesque drive across the moors to the well-known spa town of Harrogate, with its beautiful parkland and famous tearooms, where we spend the afternoon and then on to Skipton for the night. A total of 43 miles.

I expect Sunday ___will be___ (be) very tiring. Breakfast ___w___ (finish) at nine because the coach ___w___ (leave) at 9.30. We ___w___ (go) to York first. I've decided that when we ___a___ (arrive), I ___w___ (look) at the railway museum. There isn't much point in looking at the shops on a Sunday. Maybe some of the tourist shops ___w___ (be) open, but that's all. We ___w___ (have) lunch in York. After we ___have had___ (have) lunch we ___w___ (go) to Harrogate for the afternoon. We ___will___ (probably go) along the A59, so we ___w___ (go) through Knaresborough. I hope ___w___ (be able) to see the castle when we ___d___ (drive) through.

Grammar revision: comparisons

A Read the comparison of the hotels, and choose which of pictures 1 – 4 best fits the description of the Grand Hotel. Say why it is not the other hotels. Note the expressions used for comparing.

The Grand Hotel is at least 100 years older than the Hotel de Mar, and has far more character. The Grand is much more convenient for transport and the town, but it doesn't have nearly as many rooms and it isn't as luxurious. As far as entertainment is concerned, the Hotel de Mar offers much more. This is reflected in the price: the Grand is £20 per night cheaper.

B Now complete the tables of comparatives and superlatives.

Adjectives

comfortable	wore	most comfortable
cheap	cheaper	cheapest
good	better	best
worse	worse	worse
narrow	narrower	narrowest
heavy	heavier	heaviest
hard	harder	hardest
normal		

Adverbs

comfortably	more comfortably	most comfortably
cheap	more cheaply	more cheaply
well	better	best
badly	worse	badly
more narrower	more narro	most narrowly
humbly	more	more harrowly
humb		more humbly
hard	more	most
normal	more normal	most

C Tick the correct boxes and find an example of each category of comparison from the tables on page 55. For one of the categories you must tick both boxes.

	-er/-est	more/most	Example
adjectives of one syllable	☐	☐ narrow	cheaper
adjectives of two syllables:			
● ending in *y* (*y* becomes *i*)	☐	☐	normal
● ending in -*le* or -*ow*	☐	☐	_____
● other endings	☐	☐	_____
adjectives of three or more syllables	☐	☐	_____
irregular adjectives	☐	☐	good
adverbs of one syllable	eg	eg	hard
adverbs of two or more syllables	☐	☐	_____
irregular adverbs	☐	☐	comfortabl?

D Complete the gaps in the following paragraph about the Hotel de Mar. Put one word in each gap.

I would (1) _much_ rather stay in the Hotel de Mar (2) _than_ any of the other hotels. It's the best hotel (3) _of (in)_ the area. Look at it! It must be much (4) _more_ comfortable (5) _than_ the others. It's in a (6) _much_ better position, and the view is surely (7) _the_ most spectacular (8) _of_ them all. I know it's not (9) _as_ cheap (10) _as_ the one in town and it's probably (11) _more_ convenient, but if we choose this one, I'm sure we'll have (12) _less_ regrets than with any of the others.

E Choose any three of the hotels pictured on page 55 and write a paragraph comparing them and saying which one you would most like t[o] stay in and why.

Speech work: rising intonation

Main uses

Rising intonation expresses *incompleteness, uncertainty, concern*. The voice starts to rise on the last main stressed syllable and continues to rise until the end of the sentence.

a Questions requiring the answer *yes* or *no* (i.e. questions that do not start with a question word).

Did you have a good ⌣*trip?*
Was she wearing the yellow hat with a ⌣*feather in it?*

b Statements where the speaker is uncertain.

I think he said ⌣*that.*

c Questions that begin with a question word, but where the speaker wishes to emphasize concern or friendliness. Compare:

How's your ⌢*cold?*   (neutral)
How's your ⌣*cold?*   (more friendly or worried)

A Mark the last main stress in these sentences and read them aloud.

1 Did you have a good time?
2 Was your flight on time?
3 Was the hotel comfortable?
4 Was the weather good?
5 Did you manage to do much sightseeing?
6 Would you go back to the same place again?
7 Was there anything to complain about?
8 Have you planned where to go at Christmas?

In pairs, ask and answer questions 1-8 about your own holidays. Make up the details if you want to.

B Now mark the intonation on the last main stress of each sentence in the following dialogue. Then practise reading it aloud.

Functions: complaining, threatening, persuading

Martha: Did you enjoy your holiday?
Jenny: Not much. The company had overbooked the hotel and we had to stay in another one, which was much worse. [1]It was too near the centre of town and not modern enough for us.
Martha: I'm not sure, but I think you can claim compensation for that.
Jenny: Yes, [2]if they don't give me all my money back, I'm going to take them to court.
Martha: [3]Oh, come on, surely it's not worth all that trouble. [4]Wouldn't it be better to forget it?
Jenny: No, I refuse to be treated like that.

A Say whether you think each of the phrases numbered in the dialogue is formal, informal or neutral. Which functions – complaining, threatening or persuading – do the phrases express?

B In pairs, hold similar conversations about the following situations.

1 One of you has just bought a brand new car and it has just broken down.
2 One of you ate in a restaurant last night and you were very sick in the night.

C Jenny then went to the travel agent to complain and ask for some money back. With a partner, use the framework below to work out the conversation she had. Choose expressions from the lists and give reasons for choosing these expressions rather than others.

Complaining	*Threatening*	*Persuading*
I've had enough of . . .	If you don't . . ., I'll . . .	Can't you . . .
I object to . . .	Don't you dare!	I'm asking you to . . .
I want to complain . . .	If you . . ., I'll have to	Go on!
. . . is too . . .	. . .	I think you should . . .
. . . isn't . . . enough	You'll regret . . .	Are you sure you rea?ly ood that
		Look at it this way.
		Surely . . .

Jenny

| Complain about your holiday |
| Complain about the second hotel and ask for compensation. |
| Threaten to complain about him/her to head office. |
| Refuse the offer. |
| Refuse and threaten to contact your solicitor. |
| Accept and demand an answer within a week. |

Travel agent

| Try and persuade her that the second hotel was better. |
| Say that there is nothing you can do. |
| Offer her a discount on a future holiday. |
| Try and persuade her to accept it. |
| Agree to take the matter up with head office. |

EXAM FOCUS

Paper 3, Section A: cue expansion

Dos and don'ts

This part of the paper could be any one of three different types of exercise:

1 Expansion of word cues into sentences to form, usually, a letter.
2 Rewriting a passage in the form of a dialogue.
3 Completing a dialogue.

● Read the whole exercise first to get a general idea of the sense and time scale.
● Look at each verb separately and decide which tense it should be in.
● Pay attention to the fact that several words may be missing.

Make all the necessary changes and additions to make the following sentences into a letter.

Dear Hiro,
1 Your/letter/be/lovely surprise.
2 I/be/amazed/still/remember/all/time.
3 I/be/London/you/come/next month.
4 Please/give/ring/when/arrive/so/we/arrange/meet.
5 There/be/little restaurant/I/be/once/twice.
6 I/be/sure/you/love/it.
7 I/tell/Tom and Sue/you/come.
8 I/be/sure/they/like/see/you.

Regards,
Alice

Now complete the list with examples of the kinds of words which were missing.

articles: ____a____

prepositions: ____after, in, to____

conjunctions: ____when, which, or that____

pronouns: ____me, you____

modal & auxiliary verbs: ____will, can, would / have been are____

demonstrative adjectives: ____that, those, this____

Composition: informal letters

I'm looking forward to seeing you write

I'm looking forward to hearing from you

Informal letters are the ones you write to friends and relations, like the letter opposite.

A Look at this layout.

```
┌─────────────────────────┐
│                1 _____  │
│                  _____  │
│                  _____  │
│                2 _____  │
│  3 _____,               │
│  4 _____   │
│  _____   │
│  5 _____   │
│  _____   │
│  6 _____   │
│  _____   │
│  7 _____   │
│        _____            │
└─────────────────────────┘
```

1 Write your own address but *not* your name.
2 Write the day, month and year, e.g. 6th October 1989 or October 6th, 1989.
3 Use *Dear* and the name you would use when talking to the person – not *Dear Friend*.
4 First paragraph: refer to your last contact and say why you are writing.
5 Middle paragraphs: the main content of your letter.
6 Last paragraph: mention your next meeting or communication.
7 Ending: *With love* or *Regards* or *With best wishes* or *Yours* but not *Yours faithfully* or *Yours sincerely* in an informal letter.

B   See if you can find a letter hidden in this box. The first few words are done for you.

IBAWASSVERYSHUPLEASEDOCTTODEHEARFRETHATIYOUGDERAREGHYCCOMINGHETOASTAYIH
WITHDESUSREATFERLASTIKIOMHOPEGARYOUYUTIWILLGENIOYEVERYCEMINUTEB
ERFIRSTIRIWILLMAANSWERLYOURTREDBQUESTIONSYOUTUDONTDERSNEEDHAJASVISACRET
TOFIRCOMEHICHEREHBORANYUGJIINJECTIONSJIXASFORBSCLOTHESDONTTIKBBOTHERITO
BIFEBRINGTANYTHINGGUVVERYTLWARMOWASKERITBAISALWAYSOLEXTREMELYUKMNHOTATL
THISIBCSTIMETHUOFOYEARJGIHAWOULDHADVISEIVXYOUKINTOCBRINGHFSMAINLYTIKLDF
LIGHTWEIGHTTUHBCOTTONAYXCLOTHESOPANYTHINGPELSEEXOWILLBETOOLOTYHOTYONVIC
HOWEVERKDOFBRINGVIGAKOPLILIGHTUTJACKETHINASHITVJCANNIBEHRCOOLKINGETHEJO
YOMEVENINGSBAPARTFROMTHATHCTJUSTLBRINGGASDYOURSELFKITTRAVELPOLLIGHTFYOU
CANACALWAYSURTFBUYUFBORUBORROWIJNHEREYVAIMOLMREALLYCLOOKINGLOKFORWARDTO
LSEEINGNYOUFASGETKOLMINUJCTOUCHGRIFCHUMYOUUIANEEDKTOHILKNOWGDANYOPMOREB

C   Now write out the letter you found with the correct layout and punctuation, as if you are writing to a friend of yours.
Which of these titles best fits the letter? Why?

1   A friend is coming to stay for the weekend. Write to him/her explaining the arrangements.
2   A friend is coming to stay with you in your country. Write to him/her, giving the information he/she needs for the trip.
3   Write a letter to a friend inviting him/her to stay with you and telling him/her what to bring.

D   Write a letter to a classmate asking for some information which you believe he/she has. Then swap letters and reply to the one you have received.

See Activity A before you read Judy's letter.

MS not married

Dear Sir   Dear Mr Smith
Yours faithfully,   Yours
                        Sincerely
friend   best wishes
   love
with love
bye for now
See you soon

EAGLE RECREATION CENTRES
Weekend breaks in Belgium – France – Holland – Luxemburg

8th September 1987

Dear Judy

I don't know what to do. We've only been here a day, but it's all been so awful that I feel I just have to write to you and hope that you can give me some advice when I get back. I'm sending you a copy of the brochure too, so you can see what we were promised. I didn't decide to go on holiday until very late, which meant that we didn't get the tickets – or the bill! – until the actual day we left.

The first problem was my fault. So we didn't have time to sort it out with the travel agent. But they charged us for two adults instead of one adult and one child, even though Amanda is only 13. Also, they've added on an extra £5 for something, I don't know what.

We arrived here at about midday, and had to sit around for hours doing nothing because they wouldn't let us into our bungalow. And when they did eventually let us in, we found that there were no sheets or towels. We had to hire them from the park management. It's ridiculous, isn't it? Even more annoying is the fact that we've discovered that food is not included in the price, or so the management say.

On top of all that, there's a noisy disco just opposite us which carries on into the middle of the night, and the famous "South Sea Paradise" has such huge waves that I think it's dangerous, and I refuse to let Amanda swim there.

Oh dear, I am sorry to bore you with all my troubles, but I do need to talk to somebody about it. What do you think my chances are of getting the money back? We'll be returning home on Monday evening, so I hope it'll be all right if I ring you then.

With love
Bridget

finally

59

Eagle Recreation Centres in Four European Countries

Feel like a weekend break in France, Holland, Belgium or Luxemburg? Try one of the Eagle Centres, the new exciting way to take a weekend break, There's so much to do at an Eagle Recreation Centre – sport, relaxation, and lots of fun! Top of the list of attractions is the "South Sea Paradise", with its artificial all-the-year-round beach of golden sand and waving tropical palms. The water is kept at a constant 28°C, and there are waterslides, whirlpools, a wave-making machine, sauna and solarium to add to your enjoyment. When you're not relaxing in Paradise, you can enjoy the bowling alley, watersports, disco, restaurants, bars and supermarket, not to mention the indoor artificial ski-run. Accommodation is in bungalows which sleep up to 8 persons. All bungalows have full cooking facilities and colour television.

HOLIDAY PT1N (depart Fridays) includes:
- Conveyance of car (any length) and passengers via Dover or Folkstone to Boulogne, Calais or Dunkerque.
- Self-catering bungalow accomodation for 3 nights.
- All heating and lighting costs, and tourist tax.
- Royal Travellers Bond Vehicle Protection.

Prices are per person	No. of adults in car				Child 4–13
	4	3	2	1	
21.6–1.7.87 and 16.8–9.9.87	£ 76	£ 95	£ 130	£ 256	£ 12
13.9–16.12.87	69	84	114	220	12

The price covers only the accommodation and meals listed. Any additional requirements must be settled direct with the local Centre. Rooms are available for occupation from 15.00. Linen is not supplied, but may be hired on arrival. The prices for children are applicable only when a child shares with at least 2 adults. There is no charge for children under four years of age.

Bookings may be made through any branch of Fun Travel. All bookings must be accompanied by a deposit of £20 per adult. Final payments must be received 8 weeks before departure. Travel documents will be sent to you approximately 2 weeks before departure. INSURANCE – All prices include Royal Travellers Bond Vehicle Protection which provides complete insurance for the car, its passengers and contents throughout your holiday.

We are pleased to accept late bookings, but those received less than 7 days before departure will be subject to a late booking fee of £5.

Flight Information

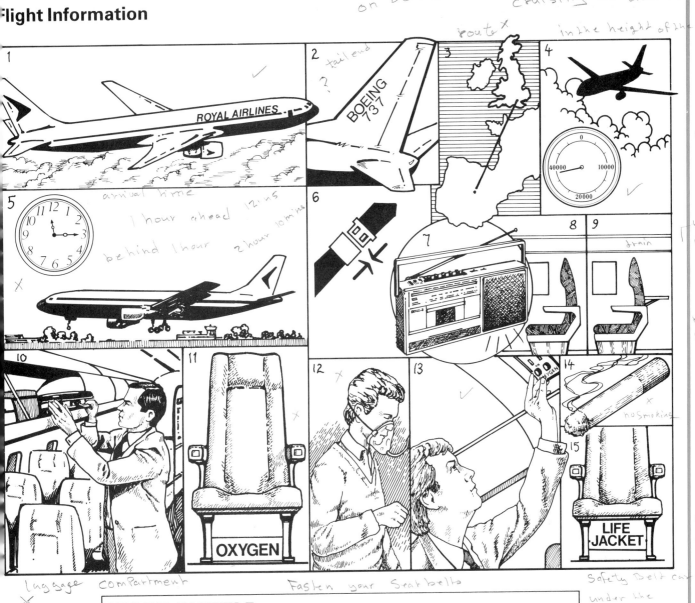

(handwritten annotations around the illustrations:) on board • cruising at 29000 ft • route • in the height of the ground • tail end • make sure that • in the upright position • arrival time • 1 hour ahead 12 ins • behind 1 hour • 2 hour 10 mins • train • reclining position • ROYAL AIRLINES • BOEING 737 • OXYGEN • no smoking • LIFE JACKET • Stowed Stow Stow • hand Luggage compartment • Fasten your seatbelts • Safety Belt can under the

WORD PUZZLE

Write the answers to the clues in the puzzle, and find a keyword down the middle. Then think up your own clue for the keyword. All the words appear in this unit.

1 Makes you sweat.
2 Leisure or relaxation.
3 Gives you information.
4 Like in the tropics.
5 Pleasure.
6 Extra.
7 What you pay first.
8 Where you dance.
9 Not natural.
10 Leaving the ground.
11 In the air.
12 A low place to live.
13 Saturday and Sunday.

Turn over for Activities

ACTIVITIES

A Recreation centre

1 Read the letter that starts *Dear Judy* on page 59, and then choose the best completion for each of these statements.
  a Bridget _____ on holiday.
    A has been   B is   C is going   D wants to go

  b A Bridget got the tickets on the day she decided to take a holiday.
    B Bridget got the tickets on the day she wrote the letter.
    C Bridget got the tickets on the day she left home.
    D Bridget didn't get the tickets at all.

  c Bridget thinks that the bill was _____.
    A too low   B too high   C just right   D too late

  d Bridget didn't have to pay extra for the _____.
    A bungalow   B food   C sheets   D towels

  e The disco _____.
    A is on top of the bungalow   C is included in the price
    B starts in the middle of the night   D is too loud

2 Down the left-hand side of a piece of paper, write headings for the seven features of the holiday that Bridget complains about. For instance:

  price
  sheets and towels

  Check your list with the person sitting next to you.

3 Read the extract from the travel brochure that describes Bridget's holiday. Each time you find something that relates to one of the headings you have written down, put a tick (✓) by the heading if you think Bridget is justified in making a complaint and a cross (x) if you think she is not. Then go through the text again and write down the reasons for your choices. For instance, if you think she is justified in her complaint about the price of the holiday, you might write:

  Price ✓ *The price for a child should have been charged for Amanda, since she is in the age group 4 to 13.*

4 **Pair work** Act out the telephone conversation between Bridget and Judy when Bridget returns from her holiday. Judy must explain why she thinks Bridget should or should not demand her money back from the travel company, Fun Travel.

5 Write one of these letters:

  ● from Judy to Bridget, answering Bridget's letter
  ● from Bridget to Fun Travel, demanding her money back
  ● from Fun Travel to Bridget, explaining why they will, or will not, pay the money back.

6 **Discussion** Look at the photograph. Are the people enjoying themselves? Do you think that the Eagle Recreation Centre would be an interesting place to have a holiday? Suggest new amenities that would make it more enjoyable.

3   Listening comprehension

1 Listen to the complete recording once, and say in as much detail as possible what the situation is. Where does it take place? Who can you hear? What time of day is it? What is the purpose of the recording?

2 Look at pictures 1-5 on page 61 and listen again to the first part of the recording, as far as . . . *local time*. Beside each number, put a tick if the picture accurately represents what is said on the tape, a cross if it is untrue, and a question mark if it is not possible to make a decision one way or the other. Listen to this section of the recording as many times as you need to.

3 Repeat the procedure with the second section of the recording, as far as. . . *exists in your area* , and pictures 6-10.

4 Repeat the procedure for the final part of the recording and pictures 11-15 .

5 Listen to the complete recording once more to check your answers.

6 Imagine that *you* are the Cabin Services Officer, and make the announcement. Use the pictures and your ticks and crosses to remind you of all the information that must be included. You do *not* need to use exactly the same words that were used in the recording.

C   Role play

1 In pairs, invent an ideal holiday resort and write a description of it for a travel brochure. Think about location, price, accommodation and amenities (restaurants, discos, etc.)

2 Put all your descriptions together to make a travel brochure, giving each holiday a code number. Study the booking form (which is taken from the brochure in which Bridget's holiday was advertised) and then compose a form of your own which better matches the holidays in your brochure; you might, for instance, not need to include details of the traveller's car and there might be other information that you think should be included on the form.

3 Act out the scene at the travel agent's. One or two students should take the parts of booking clerks, while the rest are people who plan to go on holiday.

BOOKING FORM
(Deposit payable – £20 per adult)

CLIENT'S NAME — Bridget Jones
CLIENT'S ADDRESS — 4 Garden Road
Guildford
Surrey
TEL. NO. — Guildford 632721
FUN TRAVEL BRANCH — Guildford
HOLIDAY NO. — PT1
No. of adults — 1
No. of children — 1   Ages — 13
No. of rooms — Twin/double
Singles — 3/4 bedded
Car registration no. — CPO 107L
Car make & model — Vauxhall Viva
Car height (if over 1.98m) —
Outward Route[1] — FO-BO Date 7/9/87 Time am/pm[2]
Return Route[1] — BO-FO Date 10/9/87 Time am/pm[2]
Signature — Bridget Jones
Date — 3rd Sept 1987
[1] Please use abbreviations:
HARWICH (HA), DOVER (DO), CALAIS (CA), FOLKESTONE (FO), BOULOGNE (BO), DUNKERQUE (DU)
[2] Delete as applicable.

SHOPPING AROUND

LANGUAGE STUDY

Vocabulary

Word families: money

A Fill each gap with one word taken from the cartoon. Some words will be used more than once.

1 You don't need money nowadays – you can buy on <u>credit</u> and pay later.
2 She didn't have enough money for the new car, so she took out a bank <u>loan</u>.
3 I'll never <u>lend</u> you anything again. You never give anything back.
4 It's better to <u>borrow</u> from a bank, since the <u>interest</u> is usually lower than with a <u>credit</u> card.
5 I have only two monthly <u>payment</u> left before I finish paying for my TV.
6 Put the money in an account where it will earn you some <u>interest</u>.
7 I always pay <u>cash money</u> since I hate the idea of being in debt.
8 You must pay a £500 <u>deposit</u> when you move in, in case you break anything.
9 The bank refused him a <u>mortgage</u> to buy a house, as his income was so low.
10 My brother wanted to buy my piano, so he sent me a <u>check</u> for £200.

B   Write sentences of your own, one for each of the words in the gaps.

C   In small groups, discuss the best ways to pay for these items:

> a car, a house, petrol when travelling, Christmas presents, furniture, clothes, a holiday

Phrasal verbs: *put*

D   Replace the words in italics with phrasal verbs from the list below, making any other changes necessary to keep the same meaning. Then write definitions for the phrasal verbs. (Some have more than one definition.)

1   Owing to illness the meeting was *postponed* until a week later.
2   I don't want to *inconvenience* you in any way. *Put out*
3   The visiting directors were *accommodated* in the most expensive hotel.
4   His bad luck *discouraged* me *from* starting my own business.
5   Telephone operator: 'One moment, please. I'm trying to *connect* you.'
6   The company *arranged* an exhibition of their new products. *Put on*
7   It took three hours to *extinguish* the fire. *Put out*
8   I will not *tolerate* this noise any more. *Put forward*
9   Three plans have been *suggested* for discussion. *Put forward*
10 They have *increased* the interest rate yet again.

Phrasal verbs	Definitions
put forward	Postponed
put off	discouraged
put on	arranged
put out	inconvenience
put through	connect
put up	accommodated
put up with	increased

Now write seven sentences of your own, one for each phrasal verb.

Verbs easily confused: *hire* and *rent*

● You <u>hire</u> something for one occasion only, and make one payment only.
● You <u>rent</u> something over an extended period, and make regular payments.

Discussion

Would it be normal to *hire* or *rent* the following things?

a television	a car
a boat	a flat
a garage	an electric saw

mood

Verb review: conditionals

Read these sentences carefully. Do you understand the differences between them? How does their structure compare with conditional sentences in your own language? What is *I'd* short for in the second and third sentences?

> *If I win a lot of money, I'll put it in the bank.*   possible
> *If I won a lot of money, I'd put it in the bank.*   not possible
> *If I'd won a lot of money, I'd have put it in the bank.*
> had   If there for dinner

First conditional

Make sentences from this table.

If		present tense				will + infinitive
If	we they he	buys doesn't buy buy don't buy sell	a new car, a washing machine, some old furniture,	it we they he	will won't	save on repair bills. make some money. have any money left. regret it.

A   Write sentences starting with *If . . .* to summarise the messages of these advertisements. For example:

If you use NATURAL LOOK shampoo, your hair will be shinier.

Second conditional

B   Write sentences about the advertisements starting with *If you don't . . .* and *Unless . . .* For example:

If you don't use NATURAL LOOK shampoo, your hair will look terrible.
Unless you use NATURAL LOOK shampoo, your hair will look terrible.

Find advertisements of your own in newspapers and magazines, and write sentences with *If . . .* and *Unless . . .* to say what their messages are.

C   Make sentences from this table.

If		past tense			would + infinitive
If	I they she	could had was were	more money, drive, richer,	I they she	would wouldn't 'd	buy a Mercedes. live in a flat. be dependent on friends.

D A couple are looking for a new table, but there is something wrong with all the tables in the shop. Complete the sentences.

1 If this one ____was____ a bit bigger, it __would be__ ideal.
   could have

2 If our house ____were____ bigger, we __wouldn't__ that table.

3 If we ____had____ more space, this one ___would___ very nice.

4 If they ____had____ this in a different colour, I __would buy__ it.

disposable

biodegradable

E The picture shows a shop for sale. It is near the centre of a big city in an area which is becoming more expensive to live in. If *you* bought the shop:

1 what would you do with it?
2 how would you decorate it?
3 how would you persuade people to go there?

Third conditional

F Make sentences from the table.

If		past perfect				*would have* + past participle	
If	I she you	had hadn't 'd	taken sold bought	the house, his advice,	I she you	would have wouldn't have 'd have	lost the money. been able to afford a car.

I I have been   I would have mana

Recently a new perfume was put on the market. Very few people bought it and the company lost a lot of money. They made several mistakes:

No of quantity

Made very large quantities too soon	No special offers	decrease
Price too high	Advertisements in the wrong papers	lower Put down Price
No TV advertising	Name very difficult to pronounce	cut down
No market research	Packaging ugly	reduce

G Make sentences to say what *would have happened if . . .* For example:

If they had done some market research, they would have known what the customers wanted.

What would *you* have done about the above points if you had been managing director of the company?

General practice

H Complete the sentences with suitable conditionals.

1 I don't think it's going to rain, but if . . .
2 It was a mistake to give him the gun. If . . .
3 The sea's too rough for swimming today. If . . .
4 I haven't got time to help you. If . . .
5 I'm not your mother. But if . . .
6 Here's my phone number. If . . .
7 I missed the appointment because of you. If you . . .
8 I would love to go to China. If . . .

Grammar revision: *so* and *such, too* and *enough*

So and such

- Use *so* with adverbs and adjectives without a noun.
- Use *such* with nouns (with or without articles and adjectives).

N.B. when a noun has an article, *such* comes before the article.

He was such a tall man that his head touched the ceiling.

A Fill each gap with *so* or *such*.

1 The weather was __So__ bad that we had to stay indoors.
2 We had __Such__ bad weather that we had to stay indoors.
3 Why does he write __Such__ nonsense?
4 She sang __So__ terribly that half the audience left.
5 Smith showed __Such__ a wide range of skills that we all applauded.

Too and enough

too – adje

money – noun

tall – adjec

- *Enough* is used after adjectives and adverbs but before nouns.

I didn't buy the dress because it wasn't big enough.
I didn't buy the dress because I didn't have enough money.

- *Too* is always used before an adjective or adverb.

I didn't buy the dress because it was too expensive.
The thief ran too quickly for me to catch him.

- *Too* and *enough* are followed by *for* someone or something, but *to* do something. For example:

It's too expensive for me to buy.
There aren't enough potatoes for supper.

B Put *enough* in one gap in each sentence.

1 I didn't have __enough__ time _____ to shop around for a bargain.
2 The company failed because it wasn't __enough__ competitive _____
3 I hope I can sell my house __enough__ quickly _____.
4 We haven't got __enough__ coffee _____ for all those people.
5 He didn't work __enough__ hard _____ to pass the exam.

Rewrite each of the above sentences to include *too* instead of *enough*. For example:

I had too little time to shop around for a bargain.

C Finish each of the following sentences in such a way that it means exactly the same as the one before it. For example:

The jokes he told were so bad that the audience left.
He told <u>such bad jokes that the audience left.</u>

1 They played such beautiful music that I heard nothing else.
The music __was so be_____ that I.__
2 The house was too small for six people.
The house wasn't __big enough__.
3 The people we met were so charming that we didn't want to leave.
We met __met Such__.
4 They live such a long way away that we only see them once a year.
They live so __far away__.
5 She isn't old enough to vote.
She is too __young en__.
6 He speaks too little English to use the telephone.
He doesn't speak __enough__.
7 He made such a terrible mistake that he regretted it for many years.
The mistake he made __was so terrible__.

Speech work: repeat questions

In Unit 4 we practised some uses of rising intonation. In **repeat questions**, when you want information to be repeated or explained, a special kind of rising intonation is used: the voice starts rising from the question word and continues to rise until the end.

A: *I've just bought a pestle.*   B: <u>What</u> have you bought?
[who]   <u>What</u> did you say you'd bought?
You've bought <u>what</u>?   *[you are seeing who]*
A <u>what</u>?   *[who, when, what]*

Practise responding in all four ways to ask the speaker to repeat or explain the words in italics.

[who are you see]

1 I'm seeing my *acupuncturist* later.
2 We are going to *Mali* for Christmas. *[where are going]*
3 We're having *mackerel* for *[what]* supper. *[what]*
4 I felt it was *superfluous*. *[what did you feel]*
5 He behaved so *egotistically*. *[adverb how]*
6 I prefer the *cerise* wallpaper. *[you feel what]*
7 We're going to Rome at *Whitsun*. *[when]*
8 It only costs *ten quid*. *[How much did it costs]*

Now mark the intonation of the repeat questions in the dialogue below and practise reading it aloud.

Functions: advice and suggestions

Customer: Can you give me some *advice* about these tape-recorders, please?
Assistant: Sorry? Advice about what?
Customer: These tape-recorders. I'm thinking of buying one.
Assistant: Yes, of course. *If I were you, I would* go for this one. It's certainly the most popular. And at £100 it's very good value.
Customer: How much did you say it was?
Assistant: £100. Look, *why don't you* listen to a few of them and compare? *Let's* go into the audio room. *It's a good idea to* try both recording and playing back.
Customer: All right. Thank you.

A   Which of the phrases in italics are used for the following?
1 asking for advice _____.
2 giving advice _____.
3 making suggestions _____.

B   In pairs, hold similar conversations in the following situations:

1 One of you wants to sell a bicycle. Ask you partner for advice.
2 One of you is thinking of giving up his/her job and opening a small shop. Ask your partner for advice. *[about]*
3 One of you needs to make some money quickly. Ask for advice.

Paper 3, Section A: transformation

Dos and don'ts

In this type of question you are given a complete sentence and the first word or two of a second sentence. You must complete the second sentence so that it means exactly the same as the first one. For example:

Those shoes are too expensive for me to buy.
I haven't got enough money to buy those shoes.

● Think carefully about the meaning of the sentence. Then the answer may come to you more easily.
● Don't change the meaning of the sentence.
● Don't change more words than you have to – you will only make more mistakes.
● Try and work out what is being tested. Some of the most common points that are tested are:

Present perfect and past simple	Comparisons
Reported speech	The passive
Prepositions	The conditional
Gerund and infinitive	Forming adjectives and adverbs

These examples are all based on grammar items already practised in this book. Work out what each grammar point is before you write the answer

1 It is six months since he last wrote to me.
   He hasn't _____.
   Grammar point _____.

2 My hair needs cutting.
   I must get _____.
   Grammar point _____.

3 That supermarket isn't nearly as friendly as our corner shop.
   Our corner shop is _____.
   Grammar point _____.

4 His car was so unreliable that he sold it after six months.
   It was _____.
   Grammar point _____.

5 I have never seen such a large selection of goods.
   It is the _____.
   Grammar point _____.

6 I bought this coat many years ago.
   I have _____.
   Grammar point _____.

7 They lost a lot of money when another shop opened next door.
   If another shop _____.
   Grammar point _____.

8 In case of fire, break the glass.
   If _____.
   Grammar point _____.

Composition: formal letters

You may be asked to write a letter to a stranger about something connected with his/her work. In this case your style will have to be more formal than for the letters in Unit 4.

Layout

Look at the example layout. It is similar to that for an informal letter, except that:

1 You can add the address of the person you are writing to.
2 You should write *Dear Sir or Madam*, if you do not know the name of the person you are writing to.
  Write *Dear Mr or Mrs or Ms* (+ surname) if you know the name.
3 Good ways to begin are:
  I am writing to thank you/complain/enquire, etc. or *I would like to order/confirm/apply for*, etc.
4 Explain the facts and what you want to do, or want them to do.
5 In the last paragraph, suggest that you would like a reply, if necessary. If not, you can repeat the message of the first paragraph, e.g. *Once again, I apologise for . . .*
6 The ending must be *Yours faithfully* if you have written *Dear Sir or Madam* at the beginning, and *Yours sincerely* if you have written *Dear Mr or Mrs or Ms* (+ surname).

Sort these jumbled paragraphs into two letters. One paragraph is used in both letters. Then write out one of the letters in full, with the correct layout.

Letter 1: _____   *Letter 2:* _____

1 I used to buy these products in my local supermarket but they now no longer stock them. I would be grateful if you could send me a list of outlets as I enjoy your brand more than others.

2 I would be grateful if you could send me my money back as soon as possible. I am not interested in a replacement.

3 I am writing to enquire whether you still make your soya 'meat' products and if so where I can buy them.

4 I look forward to hearing from you.

5 I am writing to complain about some of your company's chocolate that I bought recently.

6 I bought the bar in a local delicatessen that usually sells food of a very high standard. After I had eaten at least half of it, I realised that there was a live worm which had eaten its way through to the centre of the bar. It was fortunate that I looked at that point, otherwise I would have eaten the worm. I enclose the remainder of the bar as evidence.

More practice in letter writing is given in the Activities on page 75.

When you buy something you and the seller make a contract. Even if all you do is talk! The seller – not the manufacturer – must sort out your complaint.

The law has three rules:

1 Goods must be *of merchantable quality*. This means they must be reasonably fit for their normal purpose. Bear in mind the price and how the item was described. A new item must not be broken or damaged. It must work properly. But if it is very cheap, secondhand, or a 'second', you cannot expect top quality.

2 Goods must be *as described* – on the package, a display sign, or by the seller. Shirtsleeves should not be long if marked 'short' on the box. Plastic shoes must not be called leather.

3 Goods must be *fit for any particular purpose* made known to the seller. If the shop says a glue will mend china, then it should.

All goods – including those bought in sales – are covered (food too) by the law, if bought from a <u>trader</u>: for example, from shops, in street markets, through mail order catalogues or from door-to-door sellers.

Please Note!

not working

If you are <u>entitled</u> to reject something, take it back yourself if you can. It is quicker – and you can discuss it face to face. <u>Strictly</u> speaking, the seller should collect it.

You may be able to claim extra compensation if you suffer loss because of a faulty buy. For example, when a <u>faulty</u> iron <u>ruins</u> clothes.

you can buy something

You do not have to accept a <u>credit</u> note. If you do and cannot find anything else you want, it may not be easy to get your money back later.

- ☐ Keep receipts / 2
- ☐ Oh dear! 9
- ☐ Stop using faulty goods
- ☐ Tell the shop at once 5
- ☐ Take it back yourself if you can 4
- ☐ Ask for the manager 2
- ☐ Keep calm! 1
- ☐ No luck? Go to a consumer adviser 7
- ☐ Food complaints? Go to the Environmental Health Department 8
- ☐ Goods must be as described 3
- ☐ Goods must be fit for the purpose 10
- ☐ You don't have to accept a credit note 11

If things go wrong . . .

If there is something wrong with what you buy tell the seller at once.
If any of the three rules have been broken you may be able to:

● get a cash payment to make up the difference between what you paid
  and the reduced value of the faulty item, *or*
● reject it and get your money back.

you can do your selves

If you both agree, you may get a replacement or free repair.

*Exactly what you are entitled to depends on how serious the fault is and how soon
you tell the seller.*

must expect

You are not entitled to anything if you:

● examined the item when you bought it and should have seen the
  faults
● were told about the faults
● simply change your mind about wanting it
● did the damage yourself
● got it as a present (the *buyer* must make the claim)

Turn over for Activities

ACTIVITIES

A Your rights when things go wrong

Do Activity A before reading the texts on pages 72 and 73.

1 Work in pairs. Student A has just bought a portable cassette player from the shop in which Student B is the manager.

● Student A decides which of the problems below has arisen and what he/she would like to be done about it.

● Student B decides which remedy he/she thinks is most appropriate.

● Act out the situation when A returns to the shop. Try to reach a solution acceptable to both of you.

● Swap roles, choosing another of the problems.

● **Class discussion**   What would be the fairest solution to each of the problems? Try to agree on a list of solutions, and write them down like this, for example: **a3** (meaning that problem **a** should have remedy **3**).

The problems

a You drop it as you are leaving the shop and the plastic casing cracks.

b At home, you take it out of its box for the first time, and it doesn't work at all.

c A neighbour's small child pushes the on/off button so hard that it breaks.

d When you get home, you decide that you would prefer a red one.

e Through faulty mechanism it "chews up" your favourite and most expensive music tape.

f The assistant said the case was leather. It turns out to be plastic.

g You find a deep scratch on it, two inches long.

h It works normally for two weeks and then it stops.

i You were given it as a present, but you already have one.

j It gets wet in the rain one day, and the dye runs, ruining your clothes.

The remedies

1 You get your money back.

2 You get a replacement.

3 It is repaired free of charge.

4 You get nothing at all – no replacement, no repairs, and no money back.

5 You get a cash payment representing the difference between what you paid and the real value.

6 You get extra compensation over and above the value of the original article.

2 Read the texts on pages 72 and 73. From the information there, make a list of the solutions that British Law imposes for all the problems listed above. Write them in the same way as before (**a3, b4**, etc.). Discuss your answers with the rest of the class.

3 **Group work**   The pictures on pages 72 and 73 are taken from the same brochure as the texts. The captions to the pictures have been removed and are listed separately. Can you match the pictures to the captions?

B Radio programme

1 Listen to the first part of the radio programme (stop when you hear the woman's voice) and complete the information sheet.

> **Title of programme:** _at your Service_
> **Programme's telephone number:** _01 246 8041_
> **Purpose of programme:** Gives _____ when problems arise
> with _____good_____ or _____ that listeners have
> bought.
> **Programme leader's name:** _Gwen mills_
> **Other participant's name:** _Port_
> **Other participant's occupation:** _chairman_
> of the _customer_ Aid Association

2 Listen carefully to the second part of the programme (as far as 'I've really sort of lost all that money'). Fill in as many of the details as you can on the Complaints Report Form while you listen.

3 Discuss the case you have just heard about. What are the rights and wrongs of it? What advice would you give? _one thing wrong_

4 Listen to the rest of the tape and complete as much of the form as possible. Compare the advice given with your own advice and with the law as described in the texts on pages 72 and 73.

How much ?

to make a claim
under the small claims
procedure

> **Complaints Report**
>
> Name of complainant _Symmeset_
> Age _M_ Sex (M/F) _F_
> Article purchased _2ⁿᵈ Car_
> New? ☐ Secondhand? ☑
> Price asked for _1,150_
> Price paid _1,100_
> Name of seller _____
> Trader? ☐ Private person? ☑
> Was article advertised? (Y/N) _Y_
> If so, where? _New Paper_
> Faults disclosed at time of purchase
> _immaculate_
> _____
> Faults discovered later _____
> _difficult start_
> _damage with accident_
> Present value _400_
> Estimated cost of repairs _250_
> Estimated value after repairs _750_
> Suggested course of action _____
> _you may_
> _____
> _____
> _____

5 Role play in pairs Each pair invents all the details of a consumer problem like the one in the radio programme. Then two pairs meet: one presents its problem, while the other acts as Consumer Advisors, taking notes and then giving advice. Finally, swap roles, with the second pair presenting its problem.

C Letter writing

Imagine that you have bought one of the items in the pictures on page 73. Write one of these letters:

a) to the shop where you bought it, explaining what has gone wrong and saying what you would like them to do about it

b) to the Consumer Aid Association, describing the details of the problem and asking for advice.

LANGUAGE STUDY

Vocabulary

Word families:
the arts and artists

Use the phrases below to make sentences as in the example.

writes books
Someone who writes books is an author (or a writer).

writes books	tells stories
writes novels	plays a musical instrument
writes pictures	makes sculptures
writes poems	writes plays
writes music	acts in a play or film

Look at the people in the photographs. Can you match the names with the pictures and say what the people were?

Beethoven   Maria Callas   Jean Paul Sartre   Rembrandt
Shakespeare   Marilyn Monroe

A Choose words from this list to fit the definitions below and think of a well-known example of each, if possible.

short story, novel, fable, legend, drama, play, fairy tale, poetry, rhyme, fiction.

	Word(s)	Example
1 A story of full book length.	novel	
2 A traditional story usually based on history.	legend	
3 Something written for the theatre.	play	
4 A story of around 100 pages or less.	short story	
5 Literature written in verse form.	poetry	
6 A story not based on fact, usually with a moral.	fable	
7 The art of the theatre.	drama	
8 A short piece in verse, often for children and often belonging to popular culture with no known writer.	rhyme	
9 A traditional story, often for children.	fairy tale	
10 Literature based on stories that are not true.	fiction	

Phrasal verbs: *look*

B Read the examples of *look* with different particles and say what each one means in the space on the right. Then rewrite each sentence without using the word *look*.

1 If ever you come to London, *look* me *up*. _____
2 If you don't know the meaning, *look* it *up* in the dictionary. _____
3 Business is *looking up*. We'll soon be out of trouble. _____
4 Working mothers often employ nannies to *look after* their children. _____
5 I'm really *looking forward to* seeing this play – I've heard so many good things about it. _____
6 *Look out!* There's a car coming. _____
7 If you go to the party, *look out for* Tom. He's very entertaining. _____
8 The police are *looking into* the matter very thoroughly. _____
9 They are *looking for* a black actor to play the part of Othello. _____
10 *Look in on* old Mrs Jones on your way home. She may need some help. _____

Write your own sentences with these phrasal verbs.

Compound words with *look*

Which of these words are nouns, which is a verb, which is an adjective?

look-out, onlooker, outlook, overlook, good-looking

C Use the words above to fill in the spaces below; you will need to use some of the words more than once.

1 The house has a beautiful _____ over the park.
2 Making a film in a public place soon attracts a crowd of _____.
3 The new office block _____ our garden.
4 The security guards are always keeping a _____ for intruders.
5 Once the disease has developed, the _____ is not good.
6 If you want to be successful in the film world, it helps to be _____.
7 She was _____ by casting directors for many years before she was finally discovered.
8 The castle is situated at an ideal _____ point.

Ster (handwritten)

Verb review: the passive

Macbeth	*was*	*written*	*by Shakespeare.*
subject	**correct tense of the verb** *to be*	**past participle**	**agent**

Fill in the blanks in the table.

Tense		Verb *to be*	
present simple		is	
present continuous		~~was~~ being	
past simple		were	
past continuous	**The play**	was being	**performed in London.**
present perfect		has been	
past perfect		will	
will future		will ~~playing~~	
going to future		is going to be	
conditional *would*		would be	
would have		would ~~been~~ have	

The **passive** is more common in English than in many languages. It can sometimes be avoided by using the impersonal *you* or *they*, but the use of *one* is not common in English. There are two main uses of the passive:

1 When the agent is unknown or irrelevant, i.e. when we are interested only in the action. Consequently the passive is common in technical or scientific English, in such phrases as *the mixture was heated . . . the process is repeated . . .*

2 To give more stress to a certain word by putting it at the beginning or end of the sentence. For example, *Michael gave Jane the letter* can become *Jane was given the letter* or *The letter was given to Jane* or *The letter was given by Michael.*

A Say which tense each of the sentences is in and then convert it into the passive. For example:

actor (handwritten)
Dustin Hoffman has played the lead in *Death of a Salesman.*
Tense: present perfect
The lead in Death of a Salesman *has been played by Dustin Hoffman.*

(N.B. Do not write '*by . . .*' when the agent is unknown or unnecessary.)

1 The Queen is going to open the exhibition of children's art.
Tense: _P_____
The exhibition *is going to open by the queen Queen* (handwritten)

2 The pianist played the concerto very well.
Tense: _____ed
The concerto *was playing the pianist very well by the Pia* (handwritten)

3 They are still finishing the scenery for tonight's performance.
Tense: _P_ _C_
The scenery *is being finished for tonights* (handwritten)

4 They have made many of Agatha Christie's stories into films.
5 Paul Newman would have played the part better.
6 Alfred Hitchcock directed some of the best horror films.
7 When I arrived they were performing a play in the main square.
8 I was very sorry that they had closed the theatre. *them* (handwritten)
9 The Government gives a certain amount of support to the arts.
10 The President will not attend the world première.

h. w (handwritten)

The answers to 1–10 show the two main uses of the passive. For each answer say whether the passive is used:

    a) because the agent is irrelevant or unknown

or b) to stress the agent by putting it at the end.

B Look at the picture of a play that is full of disasters. Say what is wrong using the passive in different tenses. For example:

The set has been badly built.
The actors are being booed.

Tell the person next to you about a play or a film you have seen recently. Say whether you liked it or not and why. Think about the acting, the writing, the direction, etc.: *'It was (not) very well . . .*

Grammar revision: question tags

Pronoun you she

Question tags are short questions that we often attach to the end of sentences in speech, when we want the listener to respond.

They consist of a pronoun and an auxiliary or modal verb. If the main verb already has an auxiliary or modal you use that one:

> *He doesn't play that scene very well, does he?*

Otherwise you use the auxiliary associated with the tense of the main verb:

> *The box-office opens at six, doesn't it?*
> *The evening went very well, didn't it?*

A *negative* sentence is usually followed by a *positive* tag; a *positive* sentence is followed by a *negative* tag.

Add question tags in the spaces.

H.W

Julia: You went to see the new James Bond film last night, (1) _Didn't you_?
Maggie: Yes. You've seen it, (2) ____ ? *haven't you*
Julia: Yes, I saw it a few weeks ago. *is it*
Maggie: It isn't very good, (3) _is it_?
Julia: Ah, you were a fan of Sean Connery, (4) _weren't_ ? *you*
Maggie: Well, you must admit, he'd have played the part better, (5) _hadn't_ ? *wouldn't he?*
Julia: At his age! He's over 60, (6) _isn't_ ?
Maggie: He can't be, (7) _can he_? Anyway, it wasn't only that. I thought the story was a bit silly.
Julia: Yes it was, (8) _wasn't it_? And those sharks looked a bit plastic, (9) _didn't they_?
Maggie: Surely they were real ones, (10) _weren't they_.
Julia: Of course not!

Speech work: intonation of question tags

Question tags are most often said with a falling intonation; they are not genuine questions but are used simply to start a conversation or invite the listener to respond or agree:

> *It's a nice day,* ↘ *isn't it?*
> *He isn't very helpful,* ↘ *is he?*

But sometimes question tags are used as genuine questions – to ask for information or an opinion – when the speaker is uncertain of the answer. In this case they are said with a rising intonation:

> *The director comes from somewhere in Africa,* ↗ *doesn't he?*
> *The film is about jealousy,* ↗ *isn't it?*

A rising intonation is also used to show surprise:

> *You're not serious,* ↘ *are you?*
> *I haven't won,* ↘ *have I?*

A   Look again at the dialogue in the exercise above. Some of the question tags could be said with either a rising or a falling intonation, depending on the knowledge of the speaker. But other examples only have one interpretation. Find one example in the dialogue of each of the following uses:

a The speaker is just asking the listener to agree.
b The speaker is genuinely uncertain.
c The speaker is showing surprise.

Practise saying the three examples with the right intonation.

B Working in pairs, decide how each of the questions tags in the dialogue should be said, and why. Then practise reading the dialogue aloud.

A Look at these ways of expressing opinions, agreement and disagreement. Most of them are neutral: they can be used in most situations. But two of the phrases are very formal, two are very informal. Decide whether each phrase is neutral, formal, or informal and write **N**, **F** or **I** in the boxes.

Opinions	*Agreement*	*Disagreement*	
I think . . .	☐ I agree.	☐ Yes, but . . .	☐
I feel . . .	☐ I think so too.	☐ Nonsense!	☐
In my opinion . . .	☐ Exactly.	☐ I disagree.	☐
From my point of view . .	☐ You're right.	☐ I don't agree.	☐
If you ask me . . .	☐ I know.	☐ You must be joking!	☐
I consider : . .	☐ True.	☐ I'm afraid I can't agree.	☐

B Four people are looking at a painting in an art gallery. Read their conversation aloud.

A: *I think* that painting is awful.
B: *I think so too.*
C: *I agree.*
B: *If you ask me,* the artist couldn't paint.
D: *I don't agree.* I think it's very interesting.
A: *You must be joking!*

Now replace the words in italics with other phrases from the list above. Then read your new conversation aloud.

C Get into groups of three. For each of the subjects in the list below, one of you should state an opinion. The other two should agree or disagree with the statement and say why.

1 Film censorship
2 Government support of theatres
3 Free music lessons
4 Tax on books
5 Closure of cinemas
6 Opera
7 Free entry to museums
8 Advertising on TV

D The verb *agree* can be followed by *with, to,* or *on*. Use *with, to,* or *on* to fill in the spaces.

1 I agree _____ you.
2 They haven't agreed _____ a date for the show yet.
3 Her father agreed _____ let her go to the concert.
4 The actress didn't agree _____ the director's suggestion.
5 The co-authors couldn't agree _____ a title for their new book, so they agreed _____ let the publishers decide.

81

Paper 3, Section B: information retrieval

Dos and don'ts

In this section of the examination you are required to collect information from some written material and organise it into paragraphs or dialogue form.

- Use only the information that is given to you. Do not add any of your own.
- Do not copy whole sentences from the text, but you may use the vocabulary and some phrases if you wish.
- Make a list of, or mark on the paper, the points you want to include in each paragraph and then decide on the order.
- Make sure that you haven't got too many points for the number of paragraphs. Calculate roughly how many words you have for each point.
- Think about how you are going to join the points. This exercise involves mainly listing points which are the same kind of idea. Look at Exercise B on joining ideas on page 84.

Example

Two sisters have asked if you can lend them each a book. Sarah is sixteen years old. She likes books that are based on fact, particularly if they are concerned with social history. Anything to do with the war also interests her.

Her sister Julia is twelve and likes fantasy stories about children of her own age living in a totally different environment from her own.

You have two books which you think might be suitable for them – *The Diary of Anne Frank* and *The Secret Garden* by Frances Hodgson Burnett. Read the descriptions from the covers of the books and decide which is suitable for which girl.

The Diary of Anne Frank

'I want to go on living after my death. And therefore I am grateful to God for giving me this gift . . . of expressing all that is in me.'

Thirteen year-old Anne Frank with her parents and sister and four other people went into hiding in the sealed-off back rooms of an Amsterdam office building in 1942, when the Nazi invaders intensified their persecution of Jews.

For two years they remained safe. In August 1944 they were betrayed. Anne died in the ghastly concentration camp at Belsen. All the others perished too, except her father.

Anne's astonishingly intimate diary was found by accident. With a touch of genius it records the strains of her unusual life, the problems of her unfolding womanhood, her falling in love, her unswerving faith in her religion. And it reveals the shining nobility of her spirit.

Now known and loved the world over through Stage, Screen and TV adaptations, or in translation, this touchingly human document remains timeless in its appeal.

THE SECRET GARDEN

Poor Mary! She was a forlorn, unwanted, disagreeable child when, after cholera had carried off her nurse and both parents in one day, she was brought from India to live at the great lonely house (most of it shut up) on the bleak Yorkshire moors. Wandering in the gardens, she found one that was walled in. There seemed no way to get inside it – except as the robin flew, over the wall. How she got inside and what happened to her there is the sort of magic that can still happen.

It is more than fifty years since this book was written, and many of the girls who read it when it first came out are grandmothers now, but the magic of the story never fails. Girls like it most, and between the ages of nine and fourteen. And, be warned - keep your copy carefully. You will want to go back and read it over and over again.

You should start by writing notes like this:

Paragraph 1 – for Sarah – *Diary of Anne Frank* – based on fact – about the war – social history (the way people lived during the Second World War)

Paragraph 2 – For Julia – *The Secret Garden* – fantasy story – for girls 9 to 14 – environment probably different from Julia's – book has been popular with this age group for over 50 years.

Expanding the notes

I would recommend Sarah to read *The Diary of Anne Frank*, since it is a book about actual events that took place during the war. It would also satisfy Sarah's interest in social history, as it deals with the way people lived during the Second World War. (47 words)

A   Complete the second paragraph in about 50 words, including as many as possible of the points in the *notes* above.

I would recommend Julia to read . . .

B   Recently the members of a local film society were asked to vote on what type of films they would like to see. Each of the 70 members could vote for three different categories, and the total number of votes cast is shown below. It is your task to recommend three films from the catalogue. You are not allowed to spend more than a total of £60. Complete the paragraphs below, giving reasons for your choices.

BARRACUDA
Wayne David Crawford   Jason Evers
Roberta Leighton
Directed by **Harry Kerwin**
Col   15   96 mins   **£22.00**
In the waters off a Florida coastal town the Barracuda, ordinarily passive fish, have become flesh-ripping monsters. An investigation uncovers a sinister conspiracy.

THE BARRETTS OF WIMPOLE STREET
Jennifer Jones   John Gielgud
Bill Travers   Virginia McKenna
Susan Stephen   Leslie Phillips
Directed by **Sidney Franklin**
Col   U   105 mins   **£18.00**
The bedridden Elizabeth Barrett is revitalised by her love for Robert Browning and defies her tyrannical father.

THE BIBLE... IN THE BEGINNING
Richard Harris   John Huston
Ava Gardner   George C. Scott
Peter O'Toole
Directed by **John Huston**
Col   U   159 mins   **£30.00**
This film vividly recreates the events in the first part of the Book of Genesis.

BIG BAD MAMA
Angie Dickinson   William Shatner
Directed by **Steve Carver**
Col   18   85 mins   **£18.00**
The success which a widow and her two daughters achieve with bootlegging and petty theft drives them to attempt more ambitious crimes.

THE JOKERS
Michael Crawford   Oliver Reed
Directed by **Michael Winner**
Col   U   94 mins   **£18.00**
Two brothers plan a daring coup to steal the closely guarded Crown Jewels.

JUSTINE
Anouk Aimee   Dirk Bogarde
Directed by **George Cukor**
Col   18   85 mins   **£18.00**
The wife of a wealthy banker, smuggling arms to the Palestinians, uses her charms to subvert men to their political aims.

THE SELLOUT
Richard Widmark   Oliver Reed
Gayle Hunnicut   Sam Wanamaker
Directed by **Peter Collinson**
Col   15   102 mins   **£18.00**
A plot by the CIA and KGB to eliminate a double agent misfires, rekindling an ever-increasing whirlpool of violent plot and counter-plot.

THE WALKING STICK
Samantha Eggar   David Hemmings
Emlyn Williams   Francesca Annis
Directed by **Eric Till**
Col   PG   91 mins   **£18.00**
A beautiful girl, crippled by polio, falls in love with a young man, only to find that he plans to involve her in theft.

Results of poll

Film category	Votes cast
Adventure	21
Cartoons	9
Comedy	27
Crime & espionage	24
Drama	34
Musicals	17
Mystery & horror	8
Romance	29
Science fiction & fantasy	8
War	18
Westerns	15

Key

U	'Universal' viewing
15	Minimum age 15
18	Minimum age 18
PG	'Parental Guidance' (accompanied by an adult)
B/W	Black and White
Col.	Colour

Paragraph 1: The first film I recommend is . . .
Paragraph 2: The second film I recommend is . . .
Paragraph 3: Finally, I recommend . . .

Composition: discussions (1)

Dos and don'ts

- Remember to answer all parts of the question.
- Plan your composition very carefully. Sort out your ideas *before* you start to write.
- Don't let your argument become too complicated. Keep it simple.

There are four main types of composition that you might have to write:

(handwritten: home holiday)

1 The advantages and disadvantages of something.
2 A comparison between two things.
3 Your opinion on a subject and reasons for it.
4 Your opinion and suggestions on a subject.

A Say which of the four types of composition each title comes under. Some may come under more than one.

(handwritten: Censorship 2)

1 More girls than boys study <u>arts</u> subjects at universities. Say why you think this is and what might be done to change it.
2 Which do you prefer – a good novel or a good film? Why?
3 Do you think it is right that the state should be able to decide what children can see in the cinema?
4 What are the advantages and disadvantages of film censorship?
5 Some people say that violence has increased because of what people see in the cinema. Do you agree?

Could the same essay be written to answer titles **3**, **4** and **5**? If not, how would they be different?

Joining ideas

Here is a list of words and expressions that can be used to join ideas. Sor them into three groups:

1 Words that can be used for joining the same kind of idea.
2 Words that can be used for introducing a contrasting idea.
3 Words that can be used for introducing a conclusion. *(handwritten: different)*

also, on the other hand, in conclusion, in addition, however, moreover, whereas, so, in contrast, although, on balance, in the same way, therefore, firstly, secondly

B Choose from the words and phrases above to fill in the gaps.

1 <u>whereas</u> Beethoven was deaf in his later years, he still composed music.
2 Shakespeare was a great playwright. <u>moreover</u>, he was a fine poet.
3 Cézanne was more interested in form, <u>whereas</u> the impressionists were more interested in colour.
4 Aristotle was a man; all men are mortal; <u>in conclusion</u> Aristotle was mortal.
5 I like American films, <u>firstly</u>, for their realism and, <u>secondly</u> for their humour.
6 Dickens was a great novelist. His characters, <u>on other hand</u>, are sometimes a little unreal.
7 Art has caused many quarrels and even some deaths but, <u>on balance</u>, it has brought mankind more pleasure than pain.

[handwritten top left: fulfilling / rewarding]

C   Complete the sentences.

1 Work in the theatre is very badly paid. On the other hand it
It is very interesting work

2 Work in the theatre is very badly paid. Also it
It is very hard work

3 Although actors don't earn much money, they
like their job. enjoy playing) they have lots of pleasure

4 Firstly the theatre is short of money. Secondly
... they cost a lot of money to run

5 In addition to *the pays being bad*, going to the theatre is
expensive.

6 Film stars can become very rich indeed, whereas in the theatre
actor can't get a lot of money

7 An acting career has its good and bad points. On balance
he is working on a great pleasure) their work is very *satisfi...*

8 In the cinema all showings are the same. In the theatre, however,
going to the cinema is expensive (they are always chang...

9 The theatre is more expensive than the cinema. Therefore
we are going to the cinema.

10 Although *is expensive*, I still prefer the theatre.

D   Use your own ideas to fill in the spaces in this paragraph:

Learning to play the piano has some advantages. Firstly, *we learn about music*
the music. Secondly, *you can play some...*. On the other hand,
we waste time and *you can't leaving the pia...* On balance
to play to the piano is a great asset

Write similar paragraphs of your own about:

1 Becoming an actor.
2 Buying a season ticket for the local theatre.
3 Joining a library.
4 Reading reviews in newspapers.

E   Make a list of the reasons why you like:

a novels   **b** films

_____   _____
_____   _____
_____   _____
_____   _____
_____   _____

1 Write your ideas in column **a** in a paragraph of three or four sentences,
joining them with suitable words or expressions.
2 Do the same with your ideas in column **b** on a separate piece of paper.
3 Think of a suitable way of introducing the second paragraph.
4 Decide whether you really prefer novels or films and write another
paragraph, on a third piece of paper, to state your opinion and reasons
for it.
5 Put the paragraphs together to make a composition.
6 In groups of three, take paragraph one from student one, paragraph
two from student two, and so on. Put them together and see if the
composition makes sense. Be very critical. If it doesn't work, say
exactly why. Try other combinations and see if they are better or
worse.

Barbican Centre Diary

Personal and telephone booking opens **Saturday 2 November**

Priority booking before this date for Barbican Centre Mailing List Members

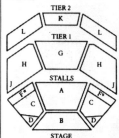

D The seats suffer limited visibility for certain performances.

F* Seats bookable in advance for wheelchair users and their escorts, and other disabled persons. Available to other patrons in person on day of performance.

G Ticket for groups of 20 or more. Adults £5.50 Students, children, OAPs £4 unless otherwise stated.

B Free Coaches to LSO promoted concerts. Se 'All about the Barbican' for details.

Y Y & M Concessionary tickets for 14–30 year olds are available at selected performances. Telephone 01-379 6722 or contact Youth & Music, 78 Neal Street, London WC2H 9PA

Sun 1 3.00 Atarah's Band

Children's and Family Fun Concert
presented by
Atarah Ben-Tovim, MBE

The best introduction to concert-going for any child. Atarah Ben-Tovim introduces a special pre-Christmas programme of music and musical fun. Music from all periods and in many styles. Children are invited to bring a recorder or simple percussion instrument, to join in under Atarah's baton.

ALL SEATS £3.50

Performance ends approx 5.00pm

Sun 1 7.30 Philharmonia Orchestra

Jan Latham-Koenig conductor
Stephen Hough piano

Rimsky-Korsakov Capriccio Espagnol
Rachmaninov Rhapsody on a Theme of Paganini
Tchaikovsky Romeo and Juliet, Fantasy Overture
Ravel Boléro

£9.80 £8.80 £7.80 £6.50
A   CG   BH   DJK

£5.50 £4
L   F*   **G**

Raymond Gubbay Ltd

Performance ends approx 9.30pm

Wed 4 7.45 London Symphony Orchestra

Brian Wright conductor
Manoug Parikian violin

Weber Overture to 'Oberon'
Vaughan Williams Fantasia on 'Greensleeves'
Bruch Violin Concerto No 1
Beethoven Symphony No 6 'Pastoral'

£8.50 £7.50 £6.50 £5.50
A   G   C   BDH

£4   £3
JKL   F*   **G**

Victor Hochhauser Ltd

Performance ends approx 9.45pm

Thu 5 7.45 Ted Heath Swing Session Christmas Special

The Ted Heath Band
Directed by **Don Lusher** with **Lita Roza** and **Dennis Lotis**
Featuring **Kenny Baker, Jack Parnell, Tommy Whittle, Duncan Campbell, Henry Mackenzie, Ronnie Chamberlain,**
with Special Guest
John Dankworth

The Ted Heath Band appears by permission of Mrs Moira Heath.

£9.50 £8   £7 £5.50 £3
ABG   CDHJ   K   L   F*

AMR Music Promotions

Performance ends approx 10.15pm

Fri 6 1.00 Guildhall Symphony Orchestra

In honour of Luciano Berio's 60th Birthday

Guildhall New Music Vocal Ensemble
John Lubbock conductor
R Strauss Waltz Sequence from 'Der Rosenkavalier'
Berio Sinfonia

ADMISSION FREE

Guildhall School of Music & Drama

Performance ends approx 1.55pm

Fri 6 7.45 City of London Sinfonia

Choir of New College, Oxford
Richard Hickox conductor
Edward Higginbottom conductor*
Gillian Fisher soprano
Lynne Dawson soprano
David James countertenor
Rogers Covey-Crump tenor
Michael George bass
John Scott organ

Vivaldi Gloria
Poulenc Christmas Motets*
Handel Organ Concerto Op 7 No 4
Bach Cantatas Nos 1 and 2 from the Christmas Oratorio

Sponsored by John Laing Construction Ltd

£8.50 £7.50 £6.50 £5.50
A   G   BCH   DJK

£4.50 £3
L   F*   **G**

City of London Sinfonia Ltd

Performance ends approx 9.45pm

Do it yourself

I can't deal with _____ got
Her kind of love is thanks a lot
You _____ happy
I'm telling you that we're not
I can't deal with _____ got

I used to have _____ life
Just working 8 till 5
She's got me _____ all the time
Trying to keep us both _____
All her fancy leather shoes
And all that make-up _____
If she don't hand me out some _____
Oh lady! We're both gonna lose

I can't deal with _____ got
Her kind of love is thanks a lot
You _____ happy
I'm telling you that I'm not
I can't deal with _____ got

When I come home _____ always cold
Your kind of cooking's making _____
So where did you get _____
Come on, sugar, _____ open a can
You're my woman, I'm your man
Oh lady! We're both _____

And now she says she says
Do it yourself, do it yourself
That's what she says she says
Do it yourself, do it yourself

We're both gonna lose

Now she says she says ...

Somebody _____ please

ACTIVITIES

A Barbican Centre

1 Scan quickly through the Barbican concert information on page 86 to find the answers to these questions.
   a On which day is a composition by Berio being performed?
   b At which concert do seats cost most?
   c Which performance ends at the latest time?
   d Which is the longest concert?
   e What word is used to mean 'people who go to a concert'?
   f In which section of the hall are the cheapest seats?
   g In which month are the concerts probably going to take place?
   h Which sections of the hall are designed for people in wheelchairs?
   i Which concerts have special prices for large groups of people?
   j To which concert should you take your own instrument?
   k Who is going to conduct 'Christmas Motets'?
   l Which concert should you go to if you enjoy piano music?
   m What is special about the concert on Friday at one o'clock?

2 Discuss the seating plan and the prices for the different sections. Which are the best/worst seats? Which section would you choose to sit in?

3 Discuss which of the advertised concerts you would enjoy going to, and give your reasons. Plan an ideal concert, listing the performers and pieces you would like to hear.

B Photograph

1 Describe the scene, the audience and the performers. What sort of place is this? What sort of music do you think they are playing?

2 Would you like to be one of the performers or a member of the audience? How do you think it feels to be on stage in front of such an audience?

3 What's your favourite form of entertainment?

C Listening

1 Listen once to the complete recording. Which word best describes the mood of the song:
   angry, *happy*, *sad* or *unsatisfied*?

2 Listen again as often as you need to, and fill in the gaps in the song lyrics.

3 **Discussion** Do you like this song? Why do you like some songs but not others? How important are these factors: the rhythm, the melody, the story or idea behind the lyrics, the singer's personality, the instruments? Think of some songs that you like and analyse why you like them.

D   Rhyme and rhythm

Pair work

Look at these advertising slogans.

Double your pleasure, double your fun   *See the USA*
With Doublemint, Doublemint, Doublemint gum!   *In your Chevrolet*

Can you make up slogans with strong rhythms and rhymes for these products?

Hornimans Tea   Marlboro cigarettes
Volvo cars   Milk
JVC tape-recorders   Weetabix breakfast cereal
Hoover washing machines   Heinz soups
TWA (airline)   Thomson Tours

E   Limericks

Limericks are five-line humorous verses with fixed patterns of rhyme and metre. Read these limericks carefully. The second one has some made up words in it – can you work out what they mean?

There was once a young lady from   Dover,   **(A)**   *rhyme*
(*di – di – da – di – di –   da – di – di – da – di*)

Who attempted to   train her dog Rover   ( )
(*di – di – da – di – di – da – di – di –   da – di*)

To   beg for his   supper.   **(B)**
(*di – da – di – di – da – di*)

But when she said 'Up!' her   ( )
(*di – da –   di – di –   da – di*)

Dim-witted companion rolled over.   ( )
(*di – da – di – di – da – di – di – da – di*)

To his offspring a parent in Sydenham   ( )   *rhyme*
Said: 'I can't find my specs; someone's hydenham.' ( )
   When in chorus they said: ( )
      'They're on top of your head!'   ( )
He tried to make out he'd been kydenham.   ( )

Pair work

1 Practise reading the limericks aloud to each other.
2 Write the letters **A** or **B** in the brackets to show the rhyming scheme.
3 Work out the metre (stress pattern) for the second limerick: write *da* under each stressed syllable and *di* under each unstressed syllable. (You will find that the two example verses are not identical in metre.)
4 Write your own limerick, starting like this:

There was once a _____
(*di –   di – da – di –*

Who _____
(*di –*

[handwritten annotations in margins: "stupid", "glasses", "kidding then", "joking", "There once was", "Fuzzy – a lot hair", "Fuzzy wuzzy was a bear", "F — had no air", "wasn't fuzzy", "was'e", "(to throw) chuck!", "How much wood"]

A Choose the best word or phrase to complete each sentence.

1 Before the invention of the motor car the _____ from London to Edinburgh took many days.
A way   B travel   C excursion   D journey

2 When you come this evening, could you _____ a corkscrew with you?
A fetch   B bring   C get   D take

3 When you _____ reading that book, can I have it back?
A have finished   B will finish   C are finishing   D are going to finish

4 I _____ to being treated like that.
A complain   B don't like   C refuse   D object

5 Don't buy the book. I'll _____ you mine.
A borrow   B lend   C rent   D hire

6 _____ you repay me immediately, I will take you to court.
A Unless   B When   C Must   D If

7 Don't worry about a hotel. We will _____ you up.
A set   B accommodate   C put   D look

8 I've just read a lovely _____ about a man who devoted his life to animals.
A fiction   B story   C history   D production

9 I _____ not agree with the Prime Minister's policies.
A am   B can't   C __   D do

10 I love classical music; _____, I rarely go to concerts.
A in addition   B therefore   C whereas   D however

11 I think access to cinemas and theatres is the main _____ of city life.
A amenity   B attraction   C leisure   D recreation

12 We shall be serving coffee immediately after _____.
A airborne   B airlift   C descent   D take-off

13 If _____ develops in your new TV within six months of purchase, . . .
A damage   B an error   C a fault   D a mistake

14 . . . you will be _____ to a replacement.
A allowed   B entitled   C guaranteed   D permitted

15 He's a very difficult person to _____ with.
A deal   B do   C get   D treat

B Finish each of the following sentences in such a way that it means exactly the same as the sentence printed before it.

1 We haven't met since 1981.
It was in 1981 that _____.

2 We didn't buy a new car because we didn't have the money.
If we _____.

3 I came to London ten years ago.
I have _____.

4 The television is still broken.
Nobody _____.

5 I was in the middle of cooking the supper when the telephone rang.
I hadn't _____

6 Work harder or you'll fail your exam.
Unless _____

7 She speaks English better than I do.
I don't _____

8 London is more expensive than other parts of the country.
Other parts of the country _____

9 I had never met a more interesting person.
He was _____

10 The writing was so terrible that I couldn't read it.
It was such _____

11 They are preparing the school for Prince Charles's visit.
The school _____

12 I haven't got a video recorder so I can't see the film.
If I _____

C   Make all the necessary changes and additions to make the following sentences into a letter.

Dear Hamish,
1 I/sorry/not/write/so/long.
2 I/work/very hard/school.
3 My course/finish/two weeks' time,/I/go/Scotland.
4 If/enough/money,/go/Ireland/as well.
5 I think/best/way/practise/English.
6 Be/possible/stay/you/couple/nights?
7 I/promise/not/be/nuisance.
8 I/even/some cooking.

Love,
Franz

D   Put *one* word in each of the numbered spaces.

It was a cold night. The train _____ (1) through some very lonely countryside. There was _____ (2) sign of human life and the station at Brest seemed _____ (3) an oasis. The passengers _____ (4) advised to get _____ (5) the train because they were going to be there _____ (6) a long time. The customs officers had to _____ (7) their duty, searching the entire train looking mainly _____ (8) illegal literature. They _____ (9) quite a lot, including some interesting magazines to _____ (10) home to their families. _____ (11) this was happening, the train moved away from the platform to _____ (12) its wheels changed. It _____ (13) lifted up and swung over on to _____ (14) wider set of wheels. But the passengers in the station did not know _____ (15) this. To them it was a long, unnecessary wait, _____ (16) worse by the fact _____ (17) their luggage disappeared with the train for at _____ (18) an hour. If they had _____ (19) given a better explanation of what was going on, they _____ (20) have been in a better mood to begin their stay in the Soviet Union.

E   Change the word in capitals to form a word that fits the space.

Example: *Measure the* _____ *and the width.*   LONG

1 I would like to book a _____ to Hong Kong.   FLY
2 I'm afraid this iron you sold me is _____.   FAULT
3 We have had a lot of _____ from customers
   today.   COMPLAIN
4 Please make your _____ at the counter over
   there.   PAY
5 Unless something is done about unemployment, the
   _____ for the future is not good.   LOOK
6 The _____ is that the plan will fail.   CONCLUDE
7 There is no _____ between the two.   COMPARE
8 I have never been _____ like that before.   THREAT

7 THE MEDIA

LANGUAGE STUDY

Vocabulary

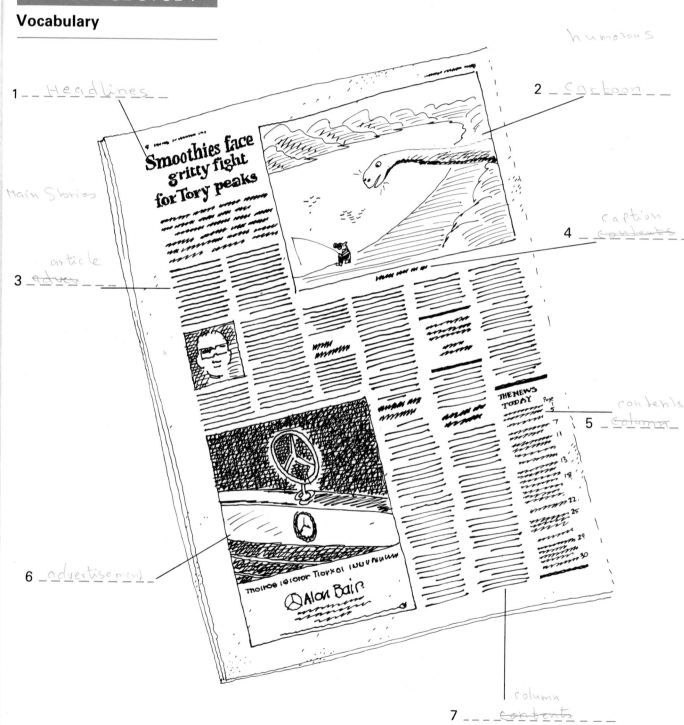

1 Headlines

Main Stories

article
3 Adver

6 advertisement

humorous
2 Cartoon

caption
4 contents

contents
5 column

column
7 contents

Word families: the news

A   Write these words in the correct places in the picture opposite.

advertisement, article, caption, cartoon, column, contents, headline

B   Put one word from the following list into each of the spaces. Make the necessary changes to the words.

announce, broadcast, print, publicise, publish

The government announced 5th
It was not Publicised

1   The Olympic Games are _broadcast_ live all over the world.
2   Winston Churchill's illness during the Second World War was not _Publicise_
3   The Government has _announce_ that the next General Election will be in June.
4   The results of the competition will be _Publish_ in the national press.
5   Millions of newspapers are _print_ every day.

a announcer
newscaster
programme Presenter
newsreader
T.J

Fill in the table to show the other forms of the words in the above list.

Publication   Publishing

Verb	Noun	Person
publish Publisher		Publisher
	Publicity	*publicist* broadcaster
broadcast	broadcasting	
announce	announcement	*announcer*
To Print	*print* Print	Printer

There are two more technical words that could be added to the list in Exercise A: *transmit* and *televise*.

Transmit means to send signals, e.g. radio or television signals.
Televise means to transmit by television.

How many other words can you think of with the prefixes *tele* and *trans*?
What do you think the prefixes mean?
Use a dictionary to help you answer these questions.

Phrasal verbs: *take*

C   Put words from the list in place of the phrasal verbs in italics in the sentences.

imitate, employ, absorb, deceive, start, remove, exhaust, resemble

1   Comedians often try to *take off* famous politicians on stage.
2   The BBC are now *taking on* more staff from ethnic minorities.
3   *Take* that hat *off*. It looks ridiculous.
4   So much information is being thrown at us that I find it hard to *take* it all *in*.
5   He *takes after* his father in the way he interviews people.
6   Working in a studio all day really *takes it out of* me.
7   I was completely *taken in* by that article. I didn't realise it was all a joke.
8   To *take up* photography as a career, you need a good camera and a lot of courage.

Write your own sentences with the phrasal verbs.

Verbs easily confused:
talk, speak, say, tell

[handwritten notes in left margin:]
she told – Pronoun
complained (P.S)   me
added   him
*   us*

She said – that

He replied
She asked
he admitted
She claimed
he maintained

D Which of the four words could you use to complete these phrases? Sometimes more than one may be possible.

1 _____ a story
2 _____ it aloud
3 _____ a lie
4 _____ to me
5 _____ something

6 _____ the truth
7 _____ English
8 _____ a word
9 _____ nonsense
10 _____ the time

Notes

Speak/talk. There is very little difference between these two words except in certain set expressions as in the exercise above. The main difference is that *speak* is more formal, whereas *talk* is more informal and conversational.

Say/tell. The most important difference is that *tell* is followed by *me, him, her, them*, etc. For example:

> *He told me his name.*
> But: *He said his name.*

Tell can also carry the meaning of an order or command. *Say* cannot. For example:

> *He told us to sit down.*

E Put the correct form of *speak, talk, say* or *tell* in the spaces.

When John _____ (1) us the news, nobody _____ (2) a word. We just couldn't _____ (3). Finally Jean _____ (4) something – I can't remember what – and somebody _____ (5) us to wait for a moment as the police wanted to _____ (6) to us. I didn't know what to _____ (7) to them. Dad has always _____ (8) us to _____ (9) nothing in such cases. I had _____ (10) enough lies in my time.

Verb review: reported speech (1)

Reported statements

[handwritten notes:]
I had gone
would
should

In **reported speech** the tenses used are usually one step back in time from the original statement, but there are some exceptions.

1 Some verb forms do not change when reported. The main ones are: past perfect, 2nd and 3rd conditionals, *used to, should, had better, ought to, might* and verbs after *wish, would rather, It's time.*

2 Often changes other than tenses have to be made. If the people reporting or receiving the reported speech are not those of the original speech, then pronouns have to be changed.
For example, Peter said to Mary:

> *I gave it to you.*

Susan reports that to John as:

> *He told her/said (that) he had given it to her.*

3 Expressions of time have to be changed when the reporting is done a long time after the original speech.
For example, last month John said to Mary:

> *I'll see you tomorrow.*

Susan would report that now to Peter as:

> *John said he would see her the next/following day.*

Reported questions

For reported questions the same tense rules as for statements apply and the word order becomes like a statement, i.e. the verb comes after the subject.
For example:

> *'Can you answer a few questions?'*
> *She asked him if he could answer a few questions.*

A Complete the table.

Original statement	Reported speech	Tense change
'I am very busy.'	He said he was very busy.	present simple → past simple
'I am leaving.'	He said _he was leaving_	present continuous → past continuous
'I arrived early.'	He said he had arrived early.	past simple → _past perfect_
'I've been here for three days.'	He said _he had been here for three days_	_____ → past perfect
'The President was expecting me.'	He said _the President had been expecting him_	_____ → _P. c_
'We've been talking all the time.'	He said _They had been talking all the time_	present perfect continuous → _____
'We'll give a press conference later.'	He said _They would be giving press conference later_	future simple → conditional
'he will see his press manager later'	He said he would be seeing his press manager later.	_____ → conditional continuous
'She will have finished her report by 6 o'clock.'	He said _She would be finished her report by 6 o'clock_	future perfect → _Past conditional continuous_

B A woman journalist is interviewing a male politician. Put the sentences into reported speech. For example:

> 'I have nothing to say.' (He said . . .)
> *He said that he had nothing to say.*

1 'How did the meeting go?' (She asked . . .)
2 'It went very well indeed.' (He told her . . .)
3 'We came to an agreement on nearly all the points.' (He explained . . .)
4 'We hope to resume talks tomorrow.' (He said . . .)
5 'What are you going to say tomorrow?' (She asked . . .)
6 'I'm afraid I can't answer that now.' (He replied . . .)
7 'Will you be able to persuade the union to accept the proposal?' (She asked . . .)
8 'It is still too early to say.' (He said . . .)
9 'I am doing everything I can.' (He added . . .)
10 'I must leave you now.' (He said . . .)

C   In pairs work out the questions you would have to ask to get the information for this questionnaire. Ask your partner the questions and make a note of her/his answers in the second column.

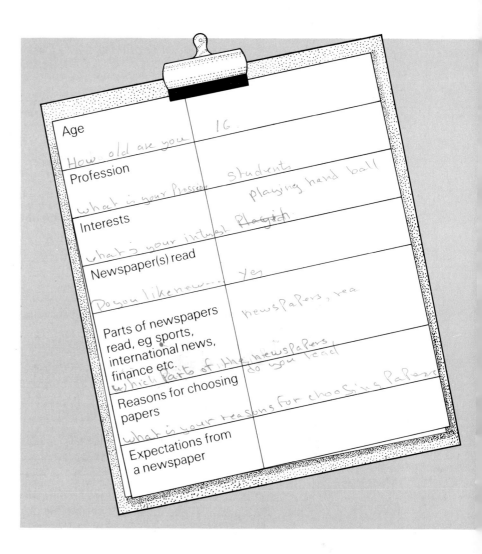

Age	16.
How old are you	
Profession	Students
what is your Profession	playing hand ball
Interests	Playgich
what is your interest Playgich	
Newspaper(s) read	Yes
Do you like new...	newspapers, rea
Parts of newspapers read, eg sports, international news, finance etc.	
which Part of the newspapers do you read	
Reasons for choosing papers	
what is your reasons for choosing Papers	
Expectations from a newspaper	

D   Now report your conversation to the rest of the class or to another pair. Begin: *When I asked her how old she was, she said . . .*

E   Here is part of a magazine report of an interview. Reconstruct the direct speech of the interview by writing the conversation like a play:

Reporter: *What are the problems of being famous?*
Miss Jay: . . .

I asked Miss Jay what the problems of being famous were. She replied that it was the lack of privacy that bothered her most and that sometimes it could get quite serious. She said that just the day before she had been sitting in a café not far from where we then were, when a man had asked her for her autograph. She said that she had signed the piece of paper he had given her without thinking. I suggested that that seemed reasonable as someone as famous as Miss Jay couldn't examine every piece of paper she was asked to autograph. She replied that that was what she had thought but she had been wrong. She explained that she had just then received a bill for five hundred pounds' worth of goods she had not bought. I asked her if she would pay the bill. She replied that she had to, because the signature on the bill was hers!

**Grammar revision:
*There is/It is***

Look at these examples:

1 *There* are several people waiting to see you.
2 Did you see the documentary on language last night? I thought *it* was very good.
3 *It* is going to rain tomorrow.
4 *It's* boring to have to sit through so many lectures.
5 *It* is through television that political parties carry out most of their campaigns.

A   Fill in the spaces with *It* or *There*, and match each of the following rules with one of the example sentences above.

1 <u>*It*</u> is used to avoid a long complicated subject before the verb. ☐
2 _____ is used to emphasise part of the sentence. ☐
3 _____ is used to refer back to something that has already been mentioned. ☐
4 _____ is used to state that something exists. ☐
5 _____ is used when there is no real subject. ☐

B   Look at these other constructions with *It* and *There*.

1 *There seems to be* a problem here.
2 *There appears to be* some mistake in my bill.
3 *There happens to be* an innocent explanation.
4 *It seems that* he was lying.
5 *It is said that* elephants never forget.
6 *It is believed that* reward is more effective than punishment.
7 *It is thought that* the Vikings first discovered America.

Write your own sentences using the phrases in italics.

C   Put *it* or *there* in each space in this letter to a newspaper.

> Dear Sir,
> _____ (1) has been a lot of discussion recently about the presentation of news on television. _____ (2) is said that _____ (3) is more violence than in the worst horror films. Is _____ (4) necessary to bring the full horror of tragic events into people's living rooms? How can children be turned away from violence if they see that the world is full of _____ (5)? For example, in Northern Ireland, _____ (6) seems to be no possibility of a normal life.
> _____ (7) is also the question of whether television is used to influence people in favour of or against a particular country or political party. _____ (8) could be very dangerous because this can happen without people realising _____ (9). Really, _____ (10) should be stricter controls on what is broadcast to the nation.
> Yours faithfully,
> Donald Scott
> Tunbridge Wells

Speech work: short vowels

Read these words aloud:

tack   tent   tick   tot   truck   took   the

Can you hear the differences between the vowel sounds?

A Practise saying these pairs. Say which of the above vowel sounds each word contains.

1 fill/fell	**7** ban/bun
2 pig/peg	**8** mad/mud
3 bit/bet	**9** dam/dumb
4 bad/bed	**10** look/lock
5 sat/set	**11** cot/cut
6 mat/met	**12** could/cud

Say one of the words above and see if your partner can point to the word you have said.

B Identify the short vowels in the dialogue and then read it aloud. Look carefully for the vowel sound you hear in *the*.

Tim: What would you like to watch on the telly tonight:?
Steve: Nothing. It's all a lot of rubbish. I just want to sit and read a book.
Tim: Good. Then I can watch whatever I want. Jim says there's a good comedy on later.
Steve: Go ahead. It's all yours.

Functions: expressing emotions

A Match these expressions with the emotions they are expressing:

1 What a shame!	☐ *Emotions*
2 What a nuisance!	☐ **a** Surprise
3 You must be joking!	☐ **b** Annoyance
4 How wonderful!	☐ **c** Pleasure
5 How irritating!	☐ **d** Disappointment
6 That's fantastic!	☐
7 That's incredible!	☐
8 Oh dear!	☐

Think of other words you could say after   *How* _____
                                            What a _____
                                            That's _____

to express different emotions.

(N.B. These are all informal expressions. A more formal way of beginning is *I find it (rather/very) disappointing, exciting, incredible, etc.*)

B In pairs, take it in turns to tell your partner what has happened. The other one should react accordingly. Here are some ideas:

1 Someone has just phoned you to say you have passed an exam.
2 Your brother has failed his driving test for the fifth time.
3 Your father has fallen and broken his leg.
4 Your purse/wallet has been stolen.
5 You've won a trip to the USA in a competition.
6 An old friend of both of you is coming to your country for a few days.
7 You can't go to the party tomorrow night because you have to baby-sit for your sister.
8 Your teacher has decided to emigrate to New Zealand.

EXAM FOCUS

Paper 3, Section A (3): completing a dialogue

Dos and don'ts

Sometimes in this part of the examination you may be asked to complete a dialogue. You will be given the words of one speaker and be asked to provide the words of the other.

- Read through the whole question before you begin. Something that comes at the end may give you some clues or vocabulary for earlier in the conversation.
- Remember to answer what was said before and lead on to what is said next.
- Note whether the conversation is formal or informal.
- Make the speech natural, with words like *well*, *anyway*, and contractions.
- Be observant. Sometimes a speaker indicates what has been said before in his answer, e.g. *Yes, I do* means there must have been a question in the present simple.

Look at the dialogue. But before completing it answer these questions:

1 What does Mr Walker want to do?
2 What are the details of what he wants?
3 What is he going to do at the end of the conversation?
4 At what points in the dialogue does Mr Walker indicate what has been said before?

Now complete the dialogue in pairs and then read your version aloud to the rest of the class.

Mr Walker: Hello, can you help me? I'd like to put an advertisement in your paper.

Mr Jones: _____

Mr Walker: My house. I'm selling my house.

Mr Jones: _____

Mr Walker: I'd like it to go in on Saturday. I think that's the day when most people have time to look, don't you?

Mr Jones: _____

Mr Walker: Well, as little as possible. I can't afford much, as the ad might have to go in for a few weeks, mightn't it?

Mr Jones: _____

Mr Walker: Oh no, just plain. I don't want a frame around it.

Mr Jones: _____

Mr Walker: OK. Can I borrow a pen to write it with, please? Twenty words doesn't sound enough, but I'll try.

Composition: discussions (2)

Dos and don'ts

- Always plan your composition before you start. Decide how many paragraphs you are going to write and what points you are going to put in each one.
- Try to make the introduction interesting. One possibility is to begin with an example.

A   Read this example of a discussion composition and say which of the titles on page 84 fits.

I heard the sound of children playing in the street outside. I listened more closely. Their words were all associated with death, injury and revenge. The names they called out were all from the latest series of so-called children's films being shown in the cinemas. They were in a fantasy world.

It could be said that these boys were playing in this way only because of the films they had seen, and that this will encourage them to grow up into violent adults.

I disagree with that. It is true that if they had not seen these films they would not be playing these particular games, but I am sure they would be playing other games of equal violence, as young boys have always done. Moreover, if allowed to get this natural violence out of their systems at an early age, they are less likely to grow up into violent adults.

To sum up, I would say that violence in the cinema does not encourage people to be violent, with the exception of a very few. However, it may give people ideas about how to put violent feelings into practice.

Write the plan that the writer of the above composition must have made.

Paragraph 1 _____

Paragraph 2 _____

Paragraph 3 _____

Paragraph 4 _____

B

1 Look at this composition title:

Do you prefer to find out what is happening in the world from television or from newspapers? Why?

Which of the essay types on page 84 is this?

2 It is quite a complicated title as it requires discussion of the advantages and disadvantages of both newspapers and television news. You need to sort out your ideas before you make your plan. Fill in this table:

Television news		Newspapers	
Advantages	Disadvantages	Advantages	Disadvantages

(Two ideas in each column are probably enough, otherwise your composition will become too involved.)

3 Now write your plan. You must decide whether it is better (a) to have one paragraph on newspapers and one on television or (b) to have one paragraph with the advantages of television and the disadvantages of newspapers and one paragraph with the reverse.

4 Now write the essay. For further practice, try compositions 1, 3 and 4 on page 84.

TV Programmes

- ☑ ARTS
- ☑ BREAKFAST TV
- ☑ CHILDREN'S
- ☑ CRICKET
- ☑ CURRENT AFFAIRS
- ☑ DRAMA
- ☑ EDUCATION
- ☑ EVENTS
- ☑ FILM
- ☑ FOOTBALL
- ☑ GARDENING
- ☑ GOLF
- ☑ LIGHT ENTERTAINMENT
- ☑ MONEY
- ☑ MUSIC
- ☑ NEWS
- ☑ POLITICS
- ☑ POP
- ☑ RACING
- ☐ RELIGION
- ☐ SCIENCE
- ☑ SNOOKER
- ☑ TENNIS
- ☑ TRAVEL
- ☑ WEATHER
- ☑ WILDLIFE

YOUR TV LICENCE IS A PERMIT TO RECEIVE ALL TELEVISION BROADCASTS

The Daily World

Monday, March 9, 1987   25p

demolished   *check hand*
at dial
transfer   **Inside Today**

. . . plus . . .

1

5

6

9

10

3

4

8

11

12

Turn over for Activities

ACTIVITIES

A TV programmes

1 What different types of programme can you watch on television? Look at page 101 and match the pictures in the leaflet with the words in the list, by writing the correct numbers in the boxes.

2 **Pair work** Tell your partner which is your favourite type of television programme, and describe a programme of this type that you have seen.

3 **Group work** Plan a whole day's television entertainment. Make a list of the programme types that should be included together with approximate times and durations. Then fill in the programme details, for instance with the programmes you have just described in Pair Work

B *The Daily World*

1 Read the newspaper contents list on page 102 Which pages would you look at if you wanted to read about the following?

a the editor's comments on the news
b recently published books
c articles for sale
d which films are being shown locally
e people who have died recently
f clothes
g tennis
h secondhand cars
i houses for sale
j news from abroad

2 **Group work** Compare the newspaper contents list with the list of television programme categories on page 101. Which categories are dealt with (1) only in the newspaper, (2) only on television, and (3) in both media. What do you think are the main reasons for the differences?

C Listening to the news

1 Read through the *Daily World* headlines on page 102. Then listen to the news broadcast and try to match the headlines with what you hear, by ticking the headlines which are dealt with in the broadcast.

2 Listen again and choose the best answer for each question.

a In the ferry disaster, most of the passengers and crew
   A are missing.   B are trapped inside.
   C have died.   D have survived.

b Which picture shows the man who was found?

A

B

C

D

c The new road in Shoreham
   A already needs repairing.
   B will avoid the town centre.
   C will demolish people's homes.
   D will not take heavy traffic.

d The teacher, George Mansfield,
   A has resigned from his job.
   B is a criminal.
   C is on strike.
   D is supported by the other teachers.

e The *South-East Courier*
   A has relied on property advertising.
   B is a free weekly newspaper.
   C will be taken over by another company.
   D is to be modernised.

f Which map shows today's weather?

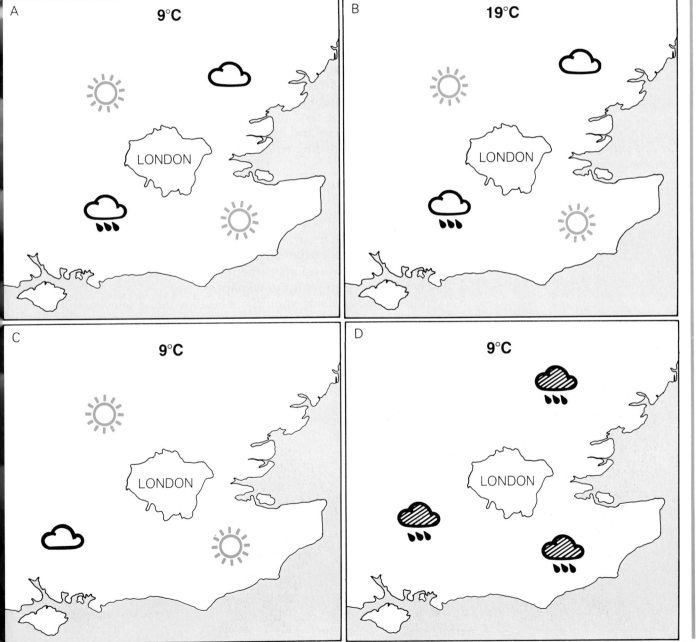

D   Discussion

1 Why do you think the news in the *Daily World* is not exactly the same as the news in the broadcast?

2 Is it important for you to keep up-to-date with the news? If so, where do you like to get news from – newspaper, radio or television?

3 What are the ingredients of a good news story?

E   News photographs

1 **Pair work**   Which of the photographs on pages 102 and 103 might illustrate the stories whose headlines are given under *Inside Today?*

2 **Group work**   Choose what you think are the two best photographs. Tell the rest of the class why you have chosen them, and give brief outlines of the stories you think they might illustrate.

3 Imagine that you have to prepare a news bulletin for broadcast on the radio.

● The class as a whole should decide:
   (i) if the broadcast is to be on local or national radio.
   (ii) which five stories of those illustrated are to be included.
● The class divides into five groups, each responsible for one story and photograph. Invent the details of the story and write down what is to be said in the broadcast. You may like to include:
   (i) live reports from the scene of the event.
   (ii) interviews with witnesses or those involved.
● One member of the class reads the news, pausing at the appropriate places for interviews and live reports. Record the broadcast, if you have access to recording equipment.

F   Written work

Write a composition of between 120 and 180 words agreeing or disagreeing with one of these statements.

1 A newspaper's best policy is to print the news that people want to read.
2 Press censorship is a necessary evil.
3 Television is a powerful instrument of social change.
4 Bad news is good news for newspapers.
5 Commercial advertising should not be allowed on television.

UNIT 8 CRIME

U N I T

LANGUAGE STUDY

Vocabulary

a

b

c

d

e

Word families:
crimes and punishments

A Which of the pictures shows:
1 a mugger?
2 a robber?
3 a pick-pocket?
4 a shoplifter?
5 a burglar?

Fill in the names of their crimes:
mugging
_____

picking pockets
_____

_____

Do you know a word which can be used for:
a all these people?
b all these crimes?

B   Match each punishment with its description:

1 a heavy fine	☐	**a**	a period in prison
2 a small fine	☐	**b**	a punishment imposed only if you
3 a prison sentence	☐		commit another crime
4 probation	☐	**c**	death
5 a suspended sentence	☐	**d**	a large sum of money to pay
6 corporal punishment	☐	**e**	a small sum of money to pay
7 capital punishment	☐	**f**	whipping or beating
		g	regular meetings with a social worker

In pairs, decide which punishment fits each crime in the pictures on page 107.

Verbs easily confused:
rob and *steal*

Look at these examples and say what the difference is between the verbs *rob* and *steal*.

> *The thieves robbed the old lady. They stole her life's savings.*
> *They robbed a bank, and stole £10,000.*

C   Put the correct form of either *rob* or *steal* in each space.

1 The post office on the High Street has been _____ again.
2 They are terrible in that shop. They _____ the public.
3 My grandmother has been _____ three times.
4 It is common practice to _____ from the government.
5 Divorced parents sometimes try to _____ their children from each other.

Phrasal verbs: *break*

D   Match the verbs in italics with the definitions. Then make your own sentences with the phrasal verbs.

1 The prisoner *broke down* and cried when the sentence was read out.
2 Six prisoners *broke out* of the local prison recently.
3 A burglar *broke into* the house next door last week.
4 The thieves were caught when their car *broke down*.
5 The police *broke* the door *down* in order to get in.
6 He *broke off* in the middle of a sentence to answer the phone.
7 The getaway car *broke through* the barrier and disappeared.
8 *Break off* a piece of that chocolate bar and give it to me.

Definitions
a come to an early end
b stop functioning properly
c escape (from a building)
d get into a locked place without a key
e detach by breaking
f lose control of one's emotions
g knock to the ground
h make a hole in something

Compound nouns with *break*

E   Put one word from the list in each of the spaces. One word is not needed.

> *breakdown, break-in, break-out, breakthrough, break-up, outbreak.*

1 There has been a _____ in communication.
2 There was a recent _____ of food-poisoning in the prison.
3 Producing test-tube babies was a medical _____.
4 Traffic was delayed because of a _____ at the crossroads.
5 There have been so many _____ in the area that the police have given up trying to find the burglars.
6 After the _____, security in the prison was tightened.

Criminal crossword

Across

1 The strongest kind of thief.
4 The person in 6 across.
6 It's not his – he _____ it.
7 The sentence was _____ long.
8 He spent _____ years in prison.
11 He saw it all.

Down

1 This is one, and it's a punishment too.
2 No one can break _____ of this place.
3 A bank _____.
5 No keys. I have to break _____ my car.
6 He was his father's _____.
8 It's OK. It's only money you have to pay.
9 A 'handy' weapon.
10 To be in debt is to _____ money.

Verb review: modals of obligation

A Replace the phrases in italics with *must, must not, have to, don't have to*.

1 I *feel it is necessary to* get an early night tonight.
2 I *am required to* be at work by 8.30 every morning.
3 We *are forbidden to* carry guns without a licence.
4 There is a collection box at the entrance to the Cathedral, but you *are not obliged to* put money in it.

B Which of the above modals best fits each definition?

1 _____ often indicates an obligation that the speaker has imposed.
   I _____ start writing my Christmas cards soon.
2 _____ often indicates an obligation imposed from outside.
   I _____ report to the police station every week.
3 _____ indicates that it is not necessary to do something, but it can be done.
   You _____ carry identity cards in Britain.
4 _____ refers to something that it is compulsory *not* to do.
   You _____ drive in the middle of the road.

Notes

● *Must* and *have to* are not very different and often it doesn't matter which you use.
● *Must* is often used in formal announcements, e.g. *Pushchairs must be folded on the escalators.*
● *Don't need to* and *needn't* are often used to mean *don't have to*.

C Make sentences using modals of obligation for each of these pictures. For example:

You mustn't smoke.

D In small groups, talk about the country you are in at the moment. Discuss the regulations concerning the following:

1 wearing seat belts
2 drinking and driving
3 wearing crash helmets
4 registering your address

5 getting married
6 voting in an election
7 identity cards
8 car accidents

Other tenses

Must can only be used in the present. For all other tenses the appropriate form of *have to* or *be allowed to* must be used.

E Complete the table.

	positive obligation	zero obligation	negative obligation	positive question
present simple	He must/has to	He doesn't have to	He mustn't	Must he?/Does he have to?
past simple	He had to		He wasn't allowed to	
present perfect				Has he had to?
past perfect				
future		He won't have to		
going to	He's going to have to			
2nd conditional				Would he have to?
3rd conditional			He wouldn't have been allowed to	

Needn't have/didn't need to

F Read these examples and answer the questions:

1 *I thought some youths were behaving suspiciously so I called the police. I later realised that I needn't have done because the boys were only playing.*

   a What needn't I have done?
   b Did I call the police?

2 *I was glad that I didn't need to report the incident because I didn't want it to get into the newspapers.*

   a Did I report the incident?
   b Why not?

What do you think is the difference between *needn't have* and *didn't have to?*

G Fill in the spaces with a suitable verb or phrase, including a modal of obligation. Sometimes more than one may be possible.

1 In future, all prisoners _____ show their letters to the guards.
2 After he had been in prison for six months, he was proved innocent. So he _____ prison.
3 If I had been found guilty, I _____ to prison.
4 Prisoners _____ in their cells; they can walk around the prison.
5 I _____ (never) _____ appear in court.
6 I _____ finish this report by tomorrow, or I'll lose my job.
7 When we came back to London, we _____ take a sword on to the plane.
8 The flight was delayed by two hours, so we _____ hurried to the airport.

Grammar revision: prepositions and gerunds

Prepositions are followed by either nouns or **gerunds** (verbal nouns ending in -*ing*).

> A knife is for **cutting** things.
> You turn it on by **pressing** the button.

Don't forget the passive and the past forms of gerunds.
> Before **being questioned** he was given drugs.
> He was ashamed of **having told** the police.

A   Complete the sentences with a suitable gerund expression.

1 After _____, he was taken to the police station.
2 Come and help me instead of _____.
3 He escaped from prison by _____.
4 In spite of _____, he was sent to prison.
5 Before _____, he asked to see his solicitor.

B   Many verbs in English are followed by a preposition and a gerund. For example:

> to accuse somebody **of doing** something

What are the prepositions that follow these verbs?

apologise _____	congratulate _____	insist _____
criticise _____	object _____	punish _____
look forward _____	blame _____	succeed _____

Write your own sentences with these verbs.

Another common construction is: the verb *to be* + adjective + preposition + gerund. For example:

> I am not very good at deceiving people.

C   Put a preposition and gerund in each space.

1 I am interested _____ people.
2 He is not very keen _____ compositions.
3 The prisoner is ashamed _____ the old lady.
4 The old lady is afraid _____ alone.
5 Many visitors to Britain are not used _____ on the left.
6 Many people are frightened _____ attacked.
7 The local police are responsible _____ the peace.
8 Many young people are bored _____ unemployed.

D   Put one word in each space.

Prisons today are sometimes criticised for _____ (1) too luxurious, and they are accused _____ (2) encouraging crime not _____ (3) it. But I have never met an ex-prisoner who is _____ (4) on _____ (5) back to prison; on the contrary, they are often very _____ (6) of being caught a second time. Yes, it was comfortable in prison, but they were most worried about not _____ (7) their families and _____ (8) their jobs. The worst punishment was the loss of freedom and no amount of luxury can compensate _____ (9) not _____ (10) allowed to walk free.

Speech work: long vowels

Read these words aloud:

> *been   burn   born   boon   barn*

Can you hear the differences between the vowel sounds?

A   Practise saying these pairs of words. The first word in each pair contains a short vowel and the second word contains a long vowel.

1 tin/teen	5 head/heard	9 spot/sport	13 pull/pool	17 ham/harm
2 hip/heap	6 ten/turn	10 pot/port	14 full/fool	18 match/march
3 fill/feel	7 west/worst	11 not/nought	15 would/wooed	19 cat/cart
4 live/leave	8 nest/nursed	12 stock/stork	16 could/cooed	20 lack/lark

Say one of the words above and see if your partner can point to the word.

B   Identify the long and short vowels in the dialogue below and read it aloud.

**Functions:
blame and apology**

Boss: Who's responsible for leaving the car park unlocked this morning?
Tim: Look, it's nothing to do with me. I wasn't even here.
Brian: No, it was my fault and I really am very sorry. It was stupid.
Boss: Well, it's OK this time, but don't let it happen in future.

Which expressions in the dialogue are used for blaming, apologising, and accepting apologies?

Which expressions in each of the lists below are (a) most formal, (b) least formal?

Blaming
The fault is mine/yours.
You are/I am to blame.
It's your/my fault.

Apologising
I (really) am very/
   terribly sorry.
I apologise for . . .
Sorry.

Accepting apologies
Not to worry.
That's OK.
That's quite all right.

Practise reading the dialogue using the alternative expressions.

Now, act out the three situations in pairs.

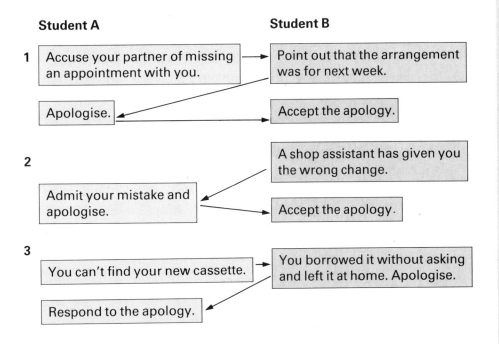

113

EXAM FOCUS

**Paper 4:
listening comprehension**

This section of the examination involves listening to three or four texts on tape and completing exercises on a printed question paper. You will hear each text twice and there will be time to study and answer the questions between each playing. The types of question will vary to include:

multiple choice questions   re-ordering
labelling/matching   blank filling
true/false selection

Dos and don'ts

● Be prepared for any type of question. You may be asked to do an exercise type that you have not done before.
● Read the instructions very carefully.
● Before the first hearing look at the questions to get a general idea of what the text is about and what information you need to listen for. Some of the information on the tape will be unnecessary for the questions.
● Don't expect to be able to answer all the questions after the first hearing. You will hear the tape again and this time you will know which parts to listen to carefully.
● Don't worry about words that you do not know. Concentrate on understanding the general sense of the text.
● Don't spend too much time worrying about a question you cannot do. You may miss the information for the questions you can do.

Radio programme: Witness

Look at the report form below, then answer these questions before listening to the tape:

1 What do you think the recording is about?
2 Which of the following do you need to listen for?
   a Information about what to do if you have seen the objects.
   b The appearance of the objects.
   c How they were stolen.
   d The history of the objects.

● Make two copies of the report form.
● Listen to the tape once and note down as much as you can. Don't worry about writing complete words at this stage.
● When the tape has finished, write down in full the information that you are sure is correct.
● Listen a second time and write down the information you missed or were not sure about the first time.

Stolen property report
Article:
Dimensions:
Colour:
Material:
Special marks:
Other distinctive features:
Condition:
Value:
Year and place of manufacture:
Date and place of theft:

**omposition:
escriptions (1)**

os and don'ts

You may be asked to describe people, objects, places or events in any type of essay, whether letters, speeches, narratives, discussions or pure descriptions. Look back at the composition titles on page 84 and say which of them include description.

● Decide what is important. You can't possibly describe *everything*. Describe the attributes which will most quickly give a clear impression of the object being described. For a person it might be sex, age, height and clothes; for a car it would be make, colour, age, size, etc.
● Choose descriptive words carefully. Vary the type of description between adjectives (*a fat man*), clauses (*a man who obviously enjoyed eating*) and similes (*he looked like an elephant*).
● Don't put too many adjectives before a noun. Two are usually enough. Instead of a *beautiful old silver dish*, write *a beautiful old dish, made of silver*.
● Keep it simple. Don't be too ambitious. Usually you will be expected to write a plain, straightforward description.

A   Read the paragraph and say which of the objects in the photograph it describes.

. . . in a simple classic style. It has black Roman numerals on a plain white face. The face is round and not cluttered with second hand or minute markings. It must have been quite expensive as it has a 9 carat gold case and a lovely soft black leather strap. The strap looks as if it has been replaced quite recently. The case is showing signs of wear.

B   Which aspects of the object are described? Write the descriptive words and phrases that belong to the following categories: age, shape, colour, material, style, texture, size, beauty, use.

C   Choose another object from the photograph and add suitable descriptive expressions for it to the chart above. Show your words to someone else in the class and see if they can guess which object you have chosen.

Forming adjectives

With suffixes like *-ish, -shaped, -like, -sounding, -looking* and *-coloured,* you can create your own adjectives.

She has a *masculine-sounding* voice.
That's a very *cheap-looking* coat.
He has bought a *rust-coloured* car.

He has an *egg-shaped* head.
She has a *childlike* face.
The carpet has a *pinkish* tint.

Discuss how you could combine the following words with the suffixes. Then make your own sentences using them.

mouse   grey
strange   white
coffee   new
wedge   young
aristocratic   animal

Adjectives using numbers

D Read the examples and explain the rule for making this type of adjective.

This note is worth five pounds.   It's a *five-pound* note.
This car has two doors.   It's a *two-door car.*

Rewrite the sentences to include 'number-noun' adjectives, as in the examples.

1 The journey took three hours.
2 The meal consisted of three courses.
3 The video cassette lasts 180 minutes.
4 I saw a clover with four leaves.
5 The house cost a million dollars.
6 This bobsleigh is for two men.
7 Buy me a bag weighing two pounds.
8 I need a plug with three pins.

More compound adjectives

Here is another type of compound adjective, used particularly to describe essential, integral attributes.
A *four-legged* animal is an animal with four legs.
A *rough-sided* object is an object with rough sides.

E Make the same sort of definitions for the following.

1 _____ is a monster with two heads.
2 _____ is a hat with three corners.
3 _____ is a man with one arm.
4 _____ is a woman with a bald head.
5 _____ is a man with a broad chest.
6 _____ is a girl with fair hair.
7 _____ is a gun with two barrels.
8 _____ is a house with three bedrooms.
9 _____ is a person with a kind heart.
10 _____ is a sword with two edges.

Composition practice

F Write one of these compositions.

1 One of the articles pictured on page 115 was stolen from you recently. The police have asked you for a written description. Write the description and say under what circumstances it was stolen.
2 Look at the pictures of criminals on page 107. Imagine that you witnessed one of these crimes and have been asked by the police to give a written description of everything you saw.
3 Describe an important landmark in the place where you live, and say why it is important.

FEAR ON THE STREETS

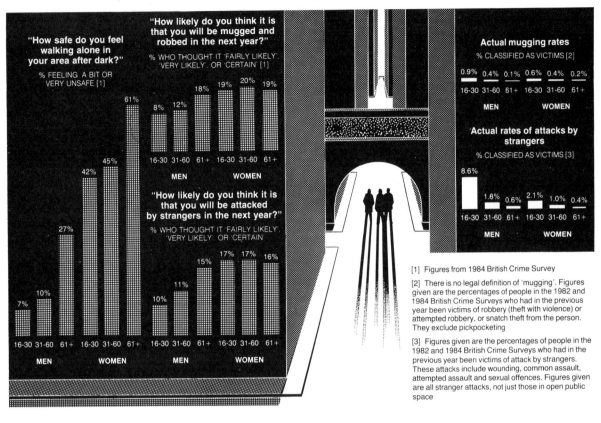

"How safe do you feel walking alone in your area after dark?"

% FEELING A BIT OR VERY UNSAFE [1]

MEN: 16-30: 7%, 31-60: 10%, 61+: 27%
WOMEN: 16-30: 42%, 31-60: 45%, 61+: 61%

"How likely do you think it is that you will be mugged and robbed in the next year?"

% WHO THOUGHT IT 'FAIRLY LIKELY', 'VERY LIKELY', OR 'CERTAIN' [1]

MEN: 16-30: 8%, 31-60: 12%, 61+: 18%
WOMEN: 16-30: 19%, 31-60: 20%, 61+: 19%

"How likely do you think it is that you will be attacked by strangers in the next year?"

% WHO THOUGHT IT 'FAIRLY LIKELY', 'VERY LIKELY' OR 'CERTAIN'

MEN: 16-30: 7%, 31-60: 10%, 61+: 27%
WOMEN: 16-30: 10%, 31-60: 11%, 61+: 15%, 17%, 17%, 16%

Actual mugging rates

% CLASSIFIED AS VICTIMS [2]

MEN: 16-30: 0.9%, 31-60: 0.4%, 61+: 0.1%
WOMEN: 16-30: 0.6%, 31-60: 0.4%, 61+: 0.2%

Actual rates of attacks by strangers

% CLASSIFIED AS VICTIMS [3]

MEN: 16-30: 8.6%, 31-60: 1.8%, 61+: 0.6%
WOMEN: 16-30: 2.1%, 31-60: 1.0%, 61+: 0.4%

[1] Figures from 1984 British Crime Survey

[2] There is no legal definition of 'mugging'. Figures given are the percentages of people in the 1982 and 1984 British Crime Surveys who had in the previous year been victims of robbery (theft with violence) or attempted robbery, or snatch theft from the person. They exclude pickpocketing

[3] Figures given are the percentages of people in the 1982 and 1984 British Crime Surveys who had in the previous year been victims of attack by strangers. These attacks include wounding, common assault, attempted assault and sexual offences. Figures given are all stranger attacks, not just those in open public space

---

'The fear of something happening to me does affect my life. I really don't like going out alone after dark and if I do, I'm always looking over my shoulder.'
(Young woman)

'I don't worry for myself but I gave my daughter an alarm and tell her to phone for me to collect her if she can't get home.' (Father)

'You read so much about muggings and so on. I don't go out in the evenings any more because I'm afraid it might happen to me.'
(Elderly woman)

Street crime in inner cities

People living in inner cities run a greater risk of being a victim than those living in other areas. They feel more vulnerable too. Even so, the fears people express are still out of proportion.

Forty five per cent of people living in inner cities said they felt a bit or very unsafe, compared with 28 per cent of people living in other areas. 1.3 per cent of people in the crime survey living in inner cities had been mugged, compared with 0.5 per cent of those living in other urban areas and 0.2 per cent in rural areas. Attacks by strangers were also more common in inner city and urban areas than in rural areas.

Increase your safety

There are no hard-and-fast rules for what to do if you are attacked; how you react will depend on the situation and on your personality. But you can take certain common-sense precautions to reduce your chances of being a victim:

● if you know you're going to be out late, think about how you'll get home beforehand, and carry enough money for a taxi just in case
● walk quickly, and look confident
● walk facing traffic, in the middle of the pavement. Avoid dimly lit short cuts
● have your keys ready when approaching your home or car
● if you think you're being followed, cross the road and change your pace to see if the person behind sticks with you. If they do, move to where you know there will be more people (a pub or busy street, say) and ask for help. Failing that, go to the nearest lit house and knock on the door
● don't have jewellery obviously on show. Gold chains, for example, can be pulled from people's necks
● carry your handbag close to your body - don't let it swing loose from your shoulder. Keep it shut, and don't leave your purse on top of a shopping bag or open handbag. Don't carry a wallet in your back pocket

● carry your keys on your person, so that if your bag is stolen the thief won't have your keys and your address. Should this happen, change your locks
● avoid empty train compartments and sit downstairs on empty buses. If possible, sit near the guard, conductor, or driver.

If you see or hear someone screaming or asking for help, DON'T ignore them. Either intervene yourself or get others to help you. Rushing off to call the police is better than nothing.

Can you hit back?

The law says you can protect yourself, but that you may use 'no more force than is necessary for mere defence. If an assault is threatened, a person may use such force as is reasonable in the circumstances to repel it'.

If someone attacked you and you managed to get them on the ground and run away, that would be self-defence and 'reasonable'. If you got them on the ground, then kicked and beat them when you could have escaped, that would not be reasonable and you could be prosecuted for assault.

It is an offence to carry a weapon that is obviously designed or adapted to cause injury – a cosh or knuckleduster, say – 'without lawful authority or resonable excuse'. *You* would have to prove you had a good reason.

Turn over for Activities

ACTIVITIES

A   Fear on the streets

1 Do *not* read the article on the previous page in detail. Glance quickly at the headings and diagrams and tick which of these topics are covered in the article.

- ☐ **a** Advice on what to do if attacked.
- ☐ **b** Advice on how to avoid being attacked.
- ☐ **c** Which are the most common crimes in Britain?
- ☐ **d** How many people expect to be attacked?
- ☐ **e** How many people are actually attacked each year?
- ☐ **f** The percentage of the population who are criminals.
- ☐ **g** Comparison of muggings in cities and rural areas.
- ☐ **h** Advice on how to report crimes.
- ☐ **i** Individuals' attitudes to mugging.
- ☐ **j** Comparison between men's and women's fears of being attacked.
- ☐ **k** Comparison between the number of attacks at night and in the daytime.
- ☐ **l** Statistics on the punishments given to muggers.

2 In pairs, choose one of the topics that you have ticked above and write a summary of all the information on these pages that relates to it. Use your own words to present the information to the rest of the class.

3 **Discussion**

a Why do you think there is such a huge difference between people's expectations of being attacked and the actual number of attacks?
b Is this a world-wide problem? How does your country compare with Britain?
c Are there any solutions to the problem of increasing crime rates?

B   Games

Fotofit

1 The teacher will give you one quarter of a photograph. All the photographs are different. Do not look at any photograph apart from the one you have been given.

2 Students should circulate in the room, describing their own pictures and listening to the other students' descriptions. The purpose of the game is to match up four segments from one picture. You *may not* look at each others' pictures until you are sure you have a complete set. The winner is the first group to match a set of pictures correctly.

Twenty questions

1 Each student brings an unusual small object to the classroom, and shows it *to no one else*.
2 One student puts his/her object into the hands of another student, who may not look at it.
3 The rest of the class must find out what the object is by asking the second student no more than twenty *yes/no* questions.
4 The student who brought the object is declared the winner if the class cannot discover what it is.
5 Repeat with another student's object.

Murder

1 Make some small squares of paper, enough for each student to have one.
2 Write the word *murderer* on one of them. Leave the remainder blank.
3 Fold all the pieces of paper so that it is impossible to see which one has been written on. Shuffle them and hand them out, one to each student.
4 Each student may look at his/her own piece of paper but at nobody else's.
5 Imagine that you are at a party. All the students should circulate in the room, making polite conversation.
6 The murderer must try to "murder" one of the students by winking at him or her, making sure that no one else can see what is happening.
7 After being winked at, the "victim" must wait at least five seconds before dying. This is to give the murderer time to mingle with the crowd.
8 When the murder has taken place, two students are appointed as detectives. Their job is to discover the identity of the murderer. They should ask questions about the guests' movements, who they were speaking to at the time of the murder, what they were talking about, and so on. They must expect the murderer to lie in order to save his or her skin.

PLAYING GAMES

Vocabulary

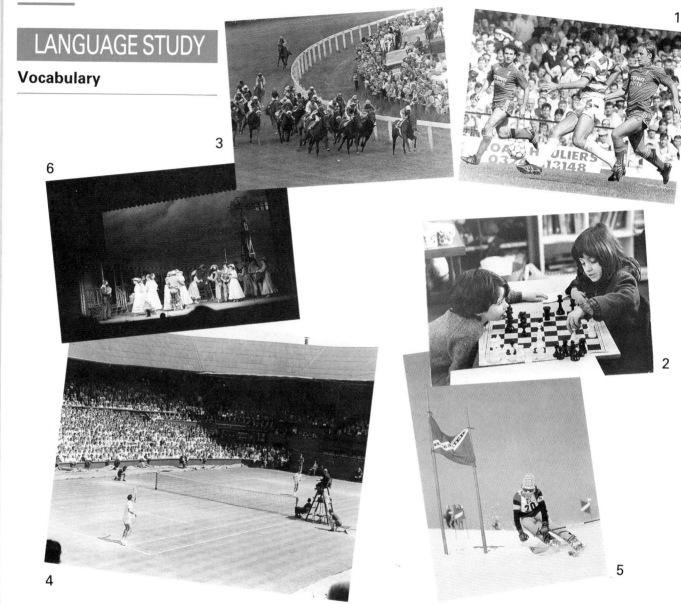

Word families:
games and matches

A Discuss the differences in meaning between the six words below, consulting a dictionary if necessary. Then match the words with the pictures above. You may have to write more than one number by some words.

a game _____   a competition _____   a match _____
a race _____   a tournament _____   a play _____

B Which noun follows which verb? Put the nouns from Exercise A after the verbs they usually follow. Some belong to more than one group.

to play: _____

to take part in: _____

Now use the nouns to describe the pictures.
For example: *In picture 2, we can see some people playing a game of chess.*

Verbs easily confused:
win and *beat*

C   Write these words after the verb which each usually follows.

the clock, a competition, a game, an opponent, a race, a prize, the system

to win: _____

to beat: _____

Which of the verbs *win* and *beat* means the same as the following?

a gain _____
b come first (in) _____
c overcome _____

D   Fill each gap with the correct form of *win* or *beat*.

1 Who _____ the match this afternoon?
2 The reigning champion has never been _____.
3 You can _____ thousands of pounds on the football pools.
4 When Scott arrived at the South Pole, Amundsen had already
  _____ him to it.
5 He did all he could to _____ her hand in marriage.

Phrasal verbs: *come*

E   Replace the words in italics with phrasal verbs from the list below, making any other changes necessary to keep the same meaning. Then write the meanings in the box. Some phrasal verbs have more than one meaning.

1 When *is* the local newspaper *published*?
2 Keep trying. I'm sure he will *be persuaded* in the end.
3 The new boys in the team are *improving* very quickly.
4 I hope the question of our poor results won't *arise* at the meeting.
5 My brother-in-law *travelled* from the USA to run in the marathon.
6 He was kicked in the head during the match, and didn't *recover consciousness* until they got him to hospital.
7 We tried to undermine our opponents' confidence, but it didn't *work*.
8 Their meeting was a strange affair. This is how it *happened* . . .
9 *Hurry up!* We're supposed to be there in five minutes.
10 He *incurred* a lot of criticism for his violence on the pitch.

Phrasal verbs	Meanings
come about	
come along	
come in for	
come off	
come on	
come out	
come over	
come round	
come to	
come up	

Write ten sentences of your own using these phrasal verbs.

Verb review: modals of possibility, deduction and ability

Possibility

Complete the table by filling in the two boxes in the right-hand column.

			do
Present simple and future		could	
Present continuous	I	might	
Past simple and present perfect		may	have done
Past continuous			

A   A politician is being interviewed about Britain's decision to withdraw from the Olympic Games. Answer the interviewer's questions in the same way as in the picture, using the correct tenses of *could, may* and *might.*

1 Is Britain likely to be disqualified from future Olympics?
2 Have the athletes been taking drugs?
3 Do you think that the money has run out?
4 Do you think that the withdrawal is only a threat?
5 Do you think the decision will lead to other countries withdrawing?
6 Are the athletes going to organise a campaign against the decision?

Deduction

*The stadium is very quiet. There **can't be** a match today. They **must be** playing tomorrow instead.*
*After last week's match, the supporters all looked very miserable, so the match **can't have been** very good: the other team **must have been** too good for us.*

B   Fill the gaps with the correct tenses of *must* and *can't,* and choose the correct forms of the verbs in brackets.

1 The stadium is very noisy. It _____ (be) an exciting match.
2 That was a loud cheer. Someone _____ (score) a goal.
3 A helicopter is flying overhead. It _____ (watch) the crowd.
4 Some supporters have blood on their faces. They _____ (fight).
5 They look very young. They _____ (be) more than sixteen.
6 The game is over, but the fans don't look happy. Their team _____ (win).
7 There are a lot of policemen around. They _____ (expect) trouble.

Ability in the past

Last year, Mandy did a course in life-saving at the local swimming pool.

1 Now she *could* save lives if anyone got into difficulties.
2 She *was able to* save her father's life when he had a heart attack in the pool.
3 She felt she *could have* saved her dog when he fell into the river.

C   Which sentence refers to:

	sentence	verb form
a an action that *was carried out*	☐	_____
b an action that *was not carried out*	☐	_____
c a *general ability*	☐	_____

Now complete the *verb form* column.

D Read the paragraph and say what the long-distance swimmer:
a could do   b was able to do   c could have done

Jim Bream is a very strong swimmer. He's never troubled by the cold, by lack of sleep or by many hours of non-stop swimming. Last year he swam across the English Channel three times, stopping only for two hours between each crossing – a total of 66 miles. He thinks the breaks were unnecessary. He wasn't tired when he finished. What about a stretch of water 66 miles across?

E Read the instructions for ®SCRABBLE and the description of this particular game. Then answer questions **1** and **2**.

Instructions

Each player has seven letters. You use them to make words, by adding them to the letters already on the board. (The number on each letter is the score you get for using that letter.) The shaded squares are bonus squares, which give you extra points. Part of the strategy of the game is to try to use the bonus squares yourself and prevent your opponents using them.

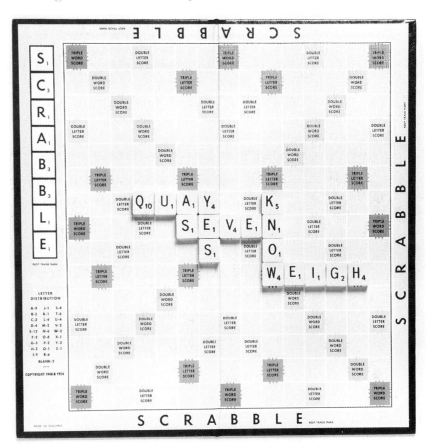

Players' letters:
Dave: OTES
Beth: LEDISEG
Clare: EARDTYZ

Three people are playing in the game you can see here. Dave has just played – he added the letters Q-U-A to the Y that was already there, and made the word QUAY. Now it is Beth's turn, and she will be followed by Clare. John is watching them play.

1 Read what John is thinking, and fill in the gaps with suitable modal verbs, as well as the correct forms of the verbs in brackets.

'I wonder why Dave did that. He _____ (use) OTES to make VOTES. That way, he _____ (use) a bonus square. He _____ (notice) it; he _____ (try) to get rid of his Q.
   Beth _____ (add) LEDGE to KNOW. But if she did that, Clare _____ (get) the bonus squares at the bottom. She _____ (try) to avoid that.
   As for Clare, well, if Beth doesn't block her, she _____ (make) GEAR, by adding EAR to the G. Then she _____ (get) the bonus square!'

2 In pairs, discuss all the possibilities for the three players.

Grammar revision: relative clauses

Non-defining relative clauses

Non-defining relative clauses add *extra* information to sentences which already make sense on their own. They are introduced by *which, where, who, whose* or *whom*. These clauses are always separated from the rest of the sentence by commas.

N.B. *Whom* is unusual in spoken English and is only really needed after a preposition,
e.g. His aunt, *with whom* he spent his childhood, has left him a fortune.

Look at these examples:

> Scrabble, *which is a word game for 2–4 players*, requires a good vocabulary.
> The centre of a cricket pitch, *where the batsmen stand*, must be kept in perfect condition.

Read the above examples without the relative clauses and you will see that they still make sense and are complete.

A   Choose the appropriate additional information about the words in italics and add it to the sentences in the form of a non-defining relative clause.

1 *John McEnroe* is an international tennis player.

2 *Chess* is very popular in the Soviet Union.

3 *Wimbledon* is in South London.

4 *Football* is a major spectator sport.

5 Every athlete's dream is to take part in the *Olympic Games*.

> *Additional information*

International tennis tournament.
Every four years.
An American.
A board game for two players.
Played all over the world.

Defining relative clauses

A defining relative clause adds *essential* information to a sentence and does *not* come between commas. Look at these sentences:

> *The player goes first.*   *This is the bat.*

Both need more information, which can be added in different ways:

The player that / who *throws the highest number goes first.*

This is the bat (that) / (which) *my uncle gave me.*

Do you know why it is possible to have no relative pronoun in the second example but not in the first?

B Read the extract from the rules for Scrabble below and add defining clauses to the sentences so that they make sense.

Make a note of each player's score after his turn. The score value of each letter is the number at the bottom of the tile. The score value of a blank is zero.

When a player forms two or more words, each word is scored. The common letter is counted in the score for each word.

Any player who plays all seven of his tiles in a single turn scores a premium of 50 points in addition to his regular score for each word.

At the end of the game each player's score is reduced by the volume of his unplayed letters. If one player has used all of his letters, his score is increased by the value of the unplayed letters of all the other players.

1 A tile _____ scores zero.

2 A letter _____ scores twice.

3 A player _____ scores an extra 50 points.

4 The number _____ is the value of the letter.

5 The player _____ gets extra points at the end.

6 The points _____ are written down.

C In pairs, think of a game whose rules you know well and write them down. Write them in such a way that every sentence contains a relative clause. Think carefully about which clauses need commas.

Speech work: diphthongs (1)

Diphthongs are sounds which consist of two or more vowels run together.

The dipthong in *town* is like the *a* in *cat* followed by the *oo* in *good*.
The dipthong in *tone* is like the *e* in *the* followed by the *oo* in *good*.

A Choose words from this list to say aloud, and see if your neighbour can hear which ones you are saying.

ground/groaned, found/phoned, loud/load, about/a boat, now/know, howl/whole

B What are the two vowel sounds that make up the diphthongs in these words?

1 *boy* is like the __ in _____ followed by the __ in _____.
2 *buy* is like the __ in _____ followed by the __ in _____.
3 *bay* is like the __ in _____ followed by the __ in _____.

C   Practise contrasting these diphthongs with pure vowels.

1 bet/bait
2 wet/weight
3 met/mate
4 pen/pain
5 sell/sale
6 mat/might
7 sand/signed
8 bat/bite

9 sat/sight
10 rat/right
11 corn/coin
12 all/oil
13 lord/Lloyd
14 bore/boy
15 tore/toy

D   Find examples of these five diphthongs in the dialogue below and read it aloud.

**Functions:
praise and criticism**

Tony: Well done, Roy! I thought you played really well.
Roy: Thanks, Tony. It could have been better, though.
Tony: Well, your footwork was a little disappointing, but your tactics were great. I was very impressed. You can be proud of yourself.
Roy: It's nice of you to say so. Thanks.

A   Find phrases in the dialogue to add to these lists.

Praise	*Criticism*	*Accepting praise*
That was marvellous!	I found . . . poor/	I'm glad you liked it.
Great!/Fantastic!	disappointing.	Thank you (very much).
What a great/superb/	You can do better than	It's kind/good of you to
terrific game!	that.	say so.
	Oh dear!	

B   Tony and Roy know each other fairly well. How would the conversation be different if they were (a) brothers, (b) a visiting official and a player? Read the dialogue, substituting alternative phrases when necessary.

C   In pairs, act out these situations.

1 Your boss has just passed his/her driving test.
2 A friend has just lost a chess game. He/she didn't play as well as usual.
3 You have just watched a colleague win a local tennis tournament.
4 You have just seen a member of your family taking part in a play. You are surprised that he/she was so good.

EXAM FOCUS

Paper 5: photographs

Dos and don'ts

At the beginning of the interview you will be given a photograph and asked some questions about it. You may be asked to describe something in the picture and/or say what you think is happening. The conversation may then lead on to a discussion of a subject related to the picture.

● Remember that the picture is there to give a focus for a conversation. It is not a test of how much you know about the subject of the picture; it is a test of how well you can speak English.
● Say as much as you can. Never answer with just *yes* or *no*. If the picture reminds you of something, say so.
● Try to show how much vocabulary you know and that you can use a variety of grammatical structures. For example, if you are looking at a picture of a beach, don't just describe it as a beach but as a *long golden, sandy beach* or a *small, stony beach*.
● Don't be afraid to say you don't know.

A Look at the first photograph and answer the questions about it in complete sentences, with as much detail as possible.

1 What do these people seem to be doing?
2 What else could they be doing?
3 What impression do you get from the expressions on their faces?
4 Do you enjoy watching any sports?
5 Why do you think people watch sport?

B Use expressions from the list below and other similar ones to talk about the second picture.

They look as if they are . . .
On the other hand they could be . . .
I've no idea what . . .
This reminds me of . . .
This is interesting/terrible because . . .

C   Take one picture each from other units in this book and think of some questions you may be asked about it. Join up with another student and interview him/her on the picture you have chosen.

Composition: descriptions (2)

Dos and don'ts

In Unit 8 we concentrated on describing single objects and people. You may sometimes be asked to describe a whole scene or event.

● Vary your sentence structure. Try not to repeat the same kind of sentences too many times. It's a good idea to have some very short sentences among the longer ones.

● Give your impressions as well as factual descriptions. For example:

It seemed that . . ., It appeared to be . . ., It looked as if . . .

● Be careful with tenses, particularly if you are describing something in the present tense. Don't forget about the present perfect.

It has been painted recently.

A   Look at this description, try to picture the scene, and say where you think it is. Then answer the questions below.

> Excitement was growing. The stadium was slowly filling up with grandfathers, fathers and sons, all with faces full of expectation. Some were listening to the radio through their headphones, others were chatting eagerly about the last match. Little boys were clutching their fathers' hands, terrified of getting lost in the crowd. There were old and young, rich and poor, black and white, all brought together by the uniform of their hats and scarves. I pitied anyone who wasn't wearing red and white that day. Their individual identities began to disappear as the time grew nearer. The ritual began. By the time the whistle blew, they were all cheering and chanting as one.

1 What tense is used mainly?
2 Why do you think this is so?
3 There are not very many adjectives. What techniques are used instead to describe the scene?
4 Notice the variety of structures and expressions used to introduce each new part of the scene. What structure is used to link 'listening to the radio' and 'chatting eagerly'? What phrase describes what the people were wearing? How are the club colours introduced? What other techniques for introducing new subjects can you find?
5 What do you notice about the sentence length?

B   Describe the scene at a sports event you have been to. Before writing:

1 Make lists of words you can use when writing about
   a the atmosphere.   b the place.   c the people.   d the sounds.

2 Decide in which order you are going to write about them, and which ones you can write about together.

Today you could WIN

Cross the BALL Jackpot

£8,250

Game 227

Near-miss Prize £100

Best Entry by an O.A.P. £50

5 Runners up Each Win £10

The jackpot this week stands at £8,250 cash. To win the jackpot the centre of the cross must coincide exactly with the centre of the erased ball. If no correct entry is received, a prize of £100 will be paid to the entrant who is nearest and £250 will be added to the next week's jackpot. Prizes will be shared by winners submitting equally correct coupons. £50 will be paid for the nearest correct entry by an OAP. Five £10 prizes will be awarded to the runners-up. When the jackpot is won no other prizes will be awarded that week.

RULES

Employees of the Southern Publishing Company (Westminster Press Ltd.) and their immediate relatives are not eligible to enter the competition.

No responsibility will be accepted for entries which are delayed, mislaid or lost and proof of posting cannot be accepted as proof of delivery.

The decision of the Editor on all matters relating to the Competition will be final. No correspondence can be entered into and the judges' decision cannot be contested.

Entries accompanied by cheque are accepted conditionally and will be disqualified if the cheque is dishonoured.

Postal orders and cheques should be made payable to SOUTHERN PUBLISHING COMPANY.

DEADLINE FOR ENTRIES

Entries must be received at our North Road, Brighton, offices by noon, Thursday or delivered to any of our branch offices or listed newsagents by 11 a.m. Wednesday.

ALL YOU HAVE TO DO

The ball has been removed from the soccer match picture. Look carefully at the position of the players.

Then use your skill by placing a cross on the coupon in ink or ball point pen at the spot you judge to be the exact centre of the ball. Crosses must not overlap. Photostat copies are not accepted.

SUPER CROSS

£1000

Now 5 chances!

As an additional bonus you can win an EXTRA £1,000 by investing in SUPERCROSSES.

For only 20p you can circle five crosses on your entry and if one is the cross that wins the Jackpot an EXTRA £1,000 is yours.

If you are a near miss winner or a runner-up, with SUPERCROSS your prize will be DOUBLED.

Turn over for Activities

	15Xs 20p		20Xs 30p		30Xs 40p		40Xs 50p		50Xs 60p		60Xs 70p		70Xs 80p		80Xs 90p		100Xs £1.00

ENTRY COUPON

Put tick against stake in appropriate box above. Minimum number of attempts 15, maximum 100. In entering the competition I agree to abide by the judges' decision.

PLEASE USE BLOCK CAPITALS

NAME ....

ADDRESS ....

....

....

GAME

Tel. No... 227

I ENCLOSE		
P/O — CHEQUE — VOUCHERS		
ENTRY FEE	SUPER X	TOTAL

Send to: CROSS THE BALL, Promotions Department, Evening Argus, 89 North Road, Brighton, BN1 4AU. Entries must be received by noon, Thursday.

The winners

STILL nobody has managed to find the magic spot, so the Jackpot goes up another £250 in Game 227 to £8,250.

Closest to dead centre of the missing ball in Game 226 was a cross submitted by Jane Winch, of South Lane, Mile End, Brighton, who wins the near-miss prize of £100. And Mr A.W. Francis, of Adelaide Square, Shoreham, takes the £50 for the best entry by an OAP.

Our five runners-up, winners of £10 each, are: Mr Giles, of Park Avenue, Eastbourne; Mr G. Wilson, of Livingstone Road, Hailsham; Mrs Joyce Bell, of Springett Avenue, Ringmer; J.D. Ramsay, of Station Road, Newhaven, and Mrs M. Wade, of Rotten Row, Lewes.

This is where the ball was in Game No. 226

ACTIVITIES

A Signals used by referees and linesmen in Association Football

☐ Direct free-kick
☐ Hand-ball
☐ Offside
☐ Start the game
☐ Foul in penalty area
☐ Indirect free-kick

☐ Player is to be
   substituted
☐ Stop the clock
☐ Foul near linesman
☐ Match nearing end
☐ Player must leave
   the field

☐ Throw-in
☐ Goal kick
☐ New ball
☐ Play on
☐ Time up

1 Listen once to the recording and identify the situation. Who are the people you can hear, and why are they there?
2 Listen to the recording again. Which signals in the pictures above are mentioned? Match them with the explanations by writing the correct numbers in the boxes. Five of the signals shown in the pictures have been invented: can you guess which they are?
3 Think of another sport, game or any other situation where special signals are used. Describe some of the signals to your partner, and see if he or she can guess what the situation is.
4 What do you think are the good and bad points of being a referee? Would you like to be a referee? Why or why not?

B Newspaper competition

1 The class should divide into five groups – **a, b, c, d** and **e**. Without reading the competition texts on pages 129 and 130 in detail, each group looks quickly for the answers to its own questions below (group **a** answers all the questions marked **a**, and so on). When you know the answers, report back to the rest of the class.

a What is the competition called?
b What is the first prize?
c What other prizes are there?
d What do you have to do?
e How many entries are allowed?

a Who is eligible to enter?
b Who won first prize in last week's competition?
c What is the name of the additional competition?
d What do you do in the additional competition?
e What does the additional competition cost?

a What does it cost to enter?
b How do you pay?
c How do you submit entries?
d What happens if entries are lost in the post?
e When must entries be submitted?

2 Read the competition texts carefully to find words that match these definitions.

a very close, but not quite hitting the target
b money prize which increases in value until won
c someone who comes second in a race or competition
d occupy the same space
e person who enters a competition or examination

f time by which something must be completed
g additional payment beyond what is due or expected
h entry form for a competition

3 In pairs, do the competition. Discuss where you think the ball might be. Remember the modal verbs:

It can't be there, because . . ., but it might be there, etc.

Then hand your entries to the teacher, who has the correct answer.

4 **Discussion** What competitions are there in magazines and newspapers that you read? In what ways are they similar to the one in this unit? Have you ever entered for a competition like this one? Why, or why not?

5 **Group work** Using 'Cross the Ball' as a model, think up a competition for your local newspaper and write all the material. Use the list of questions in 1 above to help you decide exactly what is needed. Make copies of the competition and ask the other members of the class to do it.

A Choose the best word or phrase to complete each sentence.

1 Get the cards out. I've just learnt a new _____.
   A game   B match   C contest   D play

2 You _____ me you were coming!
   A said   B explained   C told   D announced

3 Joe promised us he would finish by the _____ day.
   A previous   B before   C tomorrow   D following

4 _____ are not enough women in top jobs.
   A They   B Those   C These   D There

5 My bag's gone! I've been _____.
   A stolen   B robbed   C kidnapped   D thieved

6 The elderly lady broke _____ at her husband's funeral.
   A up   B down   C off   D out

7 Children _____ drive cars.
   A don't have to   B mustn't   C don't need to
   D needn't

8 I am not very _____ on going to a football match today.
   A interested   B enthusiastic   C happy   D keen

9 I am looking forward _____ you.
   A see   B seeing   C to see   D to seeing

10 Don't look at me like that – it wasn't my _____.
    A blame   B fault   C wrong   D faulty

11 Do you _____ in any sporting activities?
    A do   B make   C take part   D play

12 There's _____ of Len Deighton's new book in *The Times*.
    A an article   B an editorial   C an obituary   D a review

13 We promise not to reveal your _____ if you tell us who the
    thief is.
    A anonymity   B identification   C identity
    D personality

14 Even though Jones handled the ball, the referee told them to play
    _____.
    A off   B on   C through   D up

15 My wife was _____ the first prize.
    A awarded   B judged   C rewarded   D won

B Finish each of the following sentences in such a way that it means
   exactly the same as the sentence printed before it.

1 Someone has stolen my car!
   My car _____.

2 I can't see the play because it is sold out.
   If the play _____.

3 It was such a warm evening that we sat outside till midnight.
   The evening was _____.

4 'I will be back this evening,' she promised.
   She promised that _____.

5 'Have you seen my glasses?' he asked.
   He asked her _____.

6 I was stung on the eyelid by a bee.
A bee _____

7 I will come unless I hear from you.
If _____

8 It is possible that he didn't get your message.
He might _____

9 The firemen managed to rescue us from the burning house.
The firemen were _____

10 I asked the policeman if he knew where the nearest café was.
'Excuse me, _____

C Make all the necessary changes and additions to make the following sentences into a letter.

Dear Bill,

1 It/ages/I/hear/you.
2 Hope/everything/go/well.
3 I/write/ask/you/know/family/need/au pair.
4 My sister/18 years old/want/spend/year/England.
5 She/not mind/look/children/and/good/housework.
6 She/go/university/next year/study English.
7 Look/forward/hear/you.

                                                    Stefano

D Fill in the parts of the dialogue which are blank.

At a travel agency.

John: I was wondering if you have any last-minute bargains available.
Agent: _____
John: As soon as possible. Any time from tomorrow onwards.
Agent: _____
John: I don't mind, as long as it's hot. I can't wait to get away from this rain.
Agent: _____
John: That's cheap! But I would prefer somewhere a little further south than that, if possible.
Agent: _____
John: Oh dear, I suppose we should have booked earlier. But haven't you got anything for two weeks or even three? Otherwise it's hardly worth the trouble.
Agent: _____
John: That *is* a bargain. And just what I'm looking for! I'll take that one.

E Change the word in capitals to form a word that fits the space.

        Example: *Measure the ___length___ and the width.*   LONG

1 There is an old _____: 'Too many cooks spoil the broth.'   SAY
2 He finds it difficult to accept _____ from others.   CRITICISE
3 He is the only _____ that has not run this race before.   COMPETE
4 Taxi drivers have to have a very good _____ of the street names.   KNOW
5 Her _____ to learn languages is amazing.   ABLE

UNIT 10 FOOD AND FITNESS

LANGUAGE STUDY

Vocabulary

Word families:
food and cooking

A   Put one word from the list in each space. Some words will be used more than once.

course, cuisine, dish, food, helping, kitchen, meal, nourishment, plate

1 Indian _____ relies heavily on hot spices.
2 I've got a recipe for an exciting new _____.
3 Before I can make the pudding, I need a _____ to put it in.
4 A three _____ meal of soup, meat and dessert is enough for me.
5 We've broken six dinner _____ in one month.
6 The _____ is often the centre of the household.
7 That was delicious. Can I have a second _____?
8 Let's go out and have a Chinese _____.
9 Overcooked vegetables contain very little _____.
10 Many people are suspicious of _____ from other countries.

B   Explain the differences between the pairs of words. For example:

x *is* _____, *whereas* y *is* _____.
Both are _____, *but* _____.

1 course/helping   3 kitchen/cuisine
2 plate/dish   4 course/meal

C   In small groups, discuss the pictures of meals by answering the following questions. Use as many words as possible from the above exercises.

1 What are the differences between the three meals?
2 What kind of person do you think would eat each one?
3 Why do you think that?
4 Which one would you prefer to eat?
5 Why?
6 If you could choose your next meal from anywhere in the world at no cost and with no work, what would you have?

Phrasal verbs: *go*

D   Put one of the particles in each of the spaces. Some may be used more than once, and some sentences may use two particles.

against, in for, into, off, on, out, over, through, without

1 Go _____! Try it! I'm sure you'll like it.
2 The best time to barbecue food is after the fire has gone _____.
3 Have you ever thought of going _____ cooking professionally?
4 We'll go _____ it all again, so that you know exactly what you are doing.
5 The inspectors went _____ the hotel kitchens very thoroughly after some guests caught food poisoning.
6 You shouldn't go _____ what the boss says. She's usually right.
7 I used to love spaghetti, but after eating it every day for six months, I went _____ it.
8 If you won't eat what is offered, you'll just have to go _____.
9 If I were you, I wouldn't go _____ how it is made. You'd never eat it again.
10 You go _____ eating. I'll wait till you've finished.
11 I'll have to throw this milk away. It's gone _____.
12 What's going _____? I thought we were coming for a quiet meal.

Which sentence does this picture illustrate?

E   Match the definitions with the phrasal verbs from the sentences above.

	Phrasal verbs
1 change from liking to disliking	_____
2 continue	_____
3 inspect	_____
4 rehearse, practise	_____
5 be extinguished	_____
6 disobey	_____
7 not have something	_____
8 start (when telling someone else to start)	_____
9 investigate	_____
10 become bad	_____
11 happen	_____
12 pursue (an interest or career)	_____

Write your own sentences with these phrasal verbs.

Verbs easily confused: *check* and *control*

*Always **check** the 'sell-by' date when you buy packaged food.*
*When cooking with gas, it is very easy to **control** the temperature.*

F Put the correct word in the spaces.

_____ means to make sure something is all right.
_____ means to regulate or manipulate.

When I am on holiday, I find it very difficult to _____ (1) my weight. I _____ (2) it every day on the hotel scales and try and use a little self-_____ (3) when I go past a cake shop. When I am shopping I usually _____ (4) the calorie content of foods before I buy, but in some countries there are no government _____ (5) on labelling.

**Verb review:
infinitives and gerunds**

Remember that some verbs in English are always followed by the infinitive and others are always followed by the gerund:
  I *want to lose* weight.
  How can I *avoid putting on* weight?
There is a group of verbs which can take *either* the gerund *or* the infinitive, depending on the meaning:
  I *tried to eat* less but wasn't very successful.
  I *tried eating* less, but it didn't make any difference.
And there is a small group of verbs which can take either the gerund or the infinitive without changing the meaning:
  He *began following* the diet.
  He *began to follow* the diet.
So when you come across a new verb, it is important to learn how it is used in a sentence.

A As you read the text, underline these words and notice how they are used:

'We regret to inform you that we do not stock your size in . . .'
Is this you? If so, stop worrying and turn to us.
  Our club was set up for people who enjoy eating but who also hate being overweight. Many members have tried unsuccessfully to keep their weight down on their own; they may have tried giving up their favourite food or taking a run round the block every morning. They found that they couldn't go on doing it day after day without encouragement. It is so hard to remember to keep it up, to say 'no', especially when it means turning down something delicious or getting out of bed on a cold, wet morning. It often means living a life of misery.
  We all understand. We all remember doing the same things ourselves. We haven't forgotten struggling alone in a battle of will power.
We mean to help you to find a painless answer to your problems and then to go on to help others. You won't regret joining us. Don't stop to think. Do it now.

B Study the examples above very carefully, and then write *to do* or *doing* in the spaces, to match the definitions on the right. The first two have been done for you.

a remember ___doing___   remember that you have done something in the past

    remember ___to do___   remember that you must do something in the future

b	try _____	do something as an experiment, to see if it works
	try _____	make an attempt to do
c	mean _____	intend, plan
	mean _____	mean the same as, involve
d	go on _____	persevere, continue with an action
	go on _____	proceed to the next action, do next
e	forget _____	fail to do something because of poor memory
	forget _____	forget that you have done something
f	regret _____	be sorry because you must perform an unpleasant task*
	regret _____	wish that you had not done something
g	stop _____	break off an action
	stop _____	discontinue something in order to do something else

*used only before verbs like *say, inform,* etc.

C Fill the spaces with suitable verbs in either the infinitive or gerund.

1 Sorry, I forgot _____ low fat milk.
2 I remember _____ a pint of milk every day when I was a child.
3 He will never regret _____ a swimming pool built in his garden.
4 Try _____ vitamin supplements every day.
5 I've been trying _____ smoking for ten years.
6 Good health means _____ carefully.
7 I must remember _____ the doctor about this allergy.
8 I regret _____ that you have put on 3 kilos.
9 I mean _____ that dress by Christmas.
10 You really mustn't go on _____ so much alcohol.

Word groups

D What characteristics do the words in groups **A** and **B** have in common? Choose your answers from the list **1–4**.

A: adore, detest, dislike, enjoy, miss
Characteristics: _____
B: hope, plan, want, expect, long, would like
Characteristics: _____

1 followed by gerund
2 followed by infinitive
3 express attitude to particular events in the future
4 express general attitude

Often, verbs of similar meaning have the same structure. For example:

to try/attempt/make an effort/strive . . . to do something.

Can you think of any other groups of words with similar meanings that use the same structure? Think about the other verbs in the text on the previous page.

E Finish the sentences below to give advice to a friend who is planning a special meal for a family birthday. He/she wants to try something different but has not got much courage.

1 Stop _____.
2 Your father adores _____ something new.
3 Plan _____ one hour in advance.
4 Try _____ too complicated.
5 Make sure you enjoy _____.
6 Remember _____ everybody.
7 I remember _____ myself.

8 All this will mean _____ very hard.
9 I intend _____ early to help you.
10 I'd love _____ father's face.

Now write a letter to the same friend containing the ideas in the sentences and any others you may have.

**Grammar revision:
Neither do I, So do I**

Neither do I and *Nor do I* are other ways of saying 'I don't either'.
So do I is another way of saying 'I do too'.
Note the word order in this construction: just as in questions, the subject comes after the verb.

A   Fill in the spaces.

1 I'm learning English.	So	_____	I.
2 I don't speak Yoruba.	Neither	_____	I.
3 I can't fly.	_____	can	I.
4 I would like a holiday.	_____	_____	I.
5 I wouldn't like to work all night.	_____	would	_____.
6 I've got a lot of work to do.	So	_____	I.
7 I must do my best.	_____	_____	_____.
8 I'm going to take an examination.	_____	_____	_____.
9 I like the sunshine.	_____	do	_____.
10 I loved sweets as a child.	_____	_____	_____.

The above responses all indicate that things are the same for you as they are for the person you are speaking to. Here is a way of responding when things are not the same.

'I have lived in 20 different countries.'
'Have you? I haven't.'

B   Respond in the same way to these statements:

1 I can speak six oriental languages.
2 I would like to live at the South Pole.
3 I don't need to eat every day.
4 I'm flying to China tomorrow.
5 I had some injections yesterday.

C   Complete the sentences with information about yourself.

1 I can _____.
2 I like _____.
3 Last year I _____.
4 I would like _____.
5 I have got _____.
6 If I were rich, I'd _____.
7 If I fail the examination, I'll _____.
8 I hate _____.
9 I can't _____.
10 I'm don't like _____.

Listen to your neighbour's sentences and say whether or not the same applies to you.

**Speech work:
diphthongs (2)**

In Unit 9 we looked at five diphthongs. Here are two more, ending in the sound like the *e* of *the*.

The diphthong in *fair* begins with the *e* of *egg*.
The diphthong in *fear* begins with the *i* of *in*.

A   Practise contrasting these diphthongs with pure vowels.

bed/bared	very/vary	knee/near
shed/shared	dead/dared	bead/beard
ferry/fairy	fee/fear	bee/beer

B   Practise saying aloud words from these pairs. See if your neighbour can hear which word you are saying.

ear/air	here/hair	weary/wary
deer/dare	beard/bared	fear/fair
cheer/chair	peer/pair	steer/stare

C   Find examples in the dialogue below of the seven diphthongs in the following words: *town, tone, buy, bay, boy, fair, fear*.

Then practise reading the dialogue aloud.

**Functions:
giving, thanking,
offering, inviting**

Read the dialogue and say what you think the relationship is between the two people:

Julia: *Would you like to* join us for a beer tonight?
Anne: I would be delighted. *Thank you very much.* Where are you going?
Julia: We're going to the Hare and Hounds. Do you know it? *Here's the* address anyway.
Anne: *Thanks. And thanks again* for inviting me. *It's very kind of you.*
Julia: Not at all.

A   Put the expressions in italics in the dialogue and in the list below in the appropriate places in the table. Some expressions may go in more than one place.

Please accept . . .   *Can I offer you. . .?*
Allow me to . . .   *I would be pleased if you could . . .*
Thank you so much.   *This is for you.*
Thanks a lot.   *I am very grateful to you for . . .*
How about . . .   *Let me give you a hand.*

	Formal	**Neutral**	**Informal**
Giving			
Offering			
Inviting			
Thanking			

B   In pairs act out these situations.

1 Offer your boss a drink in a pub.
2 Invite your new neighbours in for a drink.
3 Offer to work late.
4 Offer to babysit for a friend.
5 Offer to help a friend cook the supper.

EXAM FOCUS

Paper 5: passage

Dos and don'ts

The second part of the interview will be based on a passage. You will be asked to read a short extract silently and then comment on it.

- Read the Exam Focus section in Unit 9 again. Most of the points concerning the photograph in the first part of the interview also apply to the passage.
- Don't worry about any words you do not know – just try and get a very general idea of what the passage is about. You will probably not be asked any comprehension questions.
- When reading, think about (a) where the passage may come from, (b) what the main idea behind it is.
- If the passage suggests something to you, don't be afraid to say so. It is intended to be a starting point for discussion, not a comprehension test.
- The examiner may help you if you are in difficulty by giving some words and ideas in his questions. Make sure you notice and use that help.
- Use the words in the text if you need to. If you know some alternatives and are sure they are right, use them.

A   Look at the questions, and then read the three passages in order to find the answers. There will be more than one possible answer for each passage.

1 Where do you think each of the passages could be found?
  a in a newspaper
  b on the radio
  c in a book on . . .
  d in a magazine
  e in a reference book
  f somewhere else. Where?

2 What discussion subjects does each passage suggest?
  a healthy eating
  b junk food
  c cookery
  d vegetarianism
  e other subjects. Which ones?

A

When it comes to the crunch, Britain is definitely a nation of crisp lovers. We munch our way through 5,000 million bags every year, making us second only to the USA in the crisp eating stakes.

In recent years, crisp makers have tempted our taste buds with many weird and wonderful flavours. Have you ever tried curry, bouquet garni or even sour cream and chives crisps? And you can now eat crisps with labels like 'lower fat', 'wholewheat' and 'lightly salted'. You can even buy crisps made from organically grown potatoes!

B

The potatoes should be boiled until they are just barely tender, not yet soft. Cut them up into rather small cubes and combine them with the cottage cheese, sour cream, garlic, salt and spring onions. Turn the mixture into a buttered casserole and sprinkle the grated cheddar cheese over the top. Add a little paprika and bake at 350°F for about half an hour.

C

In the countries of the Western part of the world, particularly in those of Europe and America, rice is not a very important cereal; yet it is the chief food of about half of all the people in the world. This is because enormous numbers of people who live in China, Japan and India, as well as other hot parts of Asia, live mainly on rice. Rice yields more food per acre than any other grain and Asia could not feed itself with any other crop.

B   In pairs, discuss the content and subject of each of the three passages. Which ones do you find interesting? Which ones would you like to know more about? Choose one of the passages, and tell your partner what you know about the subject.

Composition: informal speeches

Dos and don'ts

One of the composition questions in the examination may be to write the actual words you would say in a particular situation.

● Think carefully about style – it must fit the person you are speaking to and the situation. Read the section on style on page 17 again.
● As always, read the question very carefully. What you have to write may be either a complete speech or only part of a longer conversation.
● Don't write a *dialogue* unless you are specifically asked to. Normally you are asked to write a monologue with the other person a silent listener.

A   Here are the first paragraphs of two compositions. Read them carefully and then answer the questions.

> Now come on! You know you can't live on nothing but crisps and chocolates. For a start, they're not very good for your teeth, are they? The dentist certainly won't be very pleased with you. And how do you think you're going to grow up to be big and strong?

> I really don't think you should worry too much about your weight. After all, you're not very overweight and you always manage to look wonderful. Anyway, if it really does worry you, then all I can do is suggest a few things that I know have worked for other people.

1 Who do you think the words are being spoken to? Why do you think this?
2 What do you think the titles of the compositions are?
3 What are the differences in the language used to speak to a five-year-old child and a friend of your own age? List the main features here.

A five-year-old child	A friend of your own age

Write two or three more paragraphs to complete each composition.

B   Write a composition of 120–180 words on one of the following subjects:

1 A small child is coming to stay with you in your country for a while. You want to explain to him/her how the food will be different from what he/she is used to. Write what you would say to him/her.
2 A friend is visiting you for dinner and would like the recipe for the main course. Write what you would say.

Take care of your body

HEALTHIBREK

The Breakfast Cereal That tastes good And Does You Good!

Ingredients
Whole Wheat, Malt Extract, Iron, Salt, Sugar, Thiamin (B1), Riboflavin (B2), Niacin

TYPICAL NUTRITIONAL COMPOSITION BY WEIGHT	per 100g	per 40g
Energy	1400 kJ	560 kJ
	335 kcal	134 kcal
	10.5g	4.1g
Protein	2.0g	0.8g
Fat		
Available Carbohydrate	66.8g	26.5g
Dietary fibre	12.8g	5.1g
Iron	6.0mg	2.4mg

One bowlful of HEALTHIBREK provides at least one quarter of the Recommended Daily Amount (RDA) of these vitamins:

	Quantity per 40g serving	
Niacin	4.45mg	25% RDA
Thiamin (B1)	0.32mg	27% RDA
Riboflavin (B2)	0.48mg	30% RDA

Protein is important because it helps to build up and regenerate the cells of the body, e.g. the muscles.
Vitamin B helps your body break down your food. It is also good for the skin, hair, nails, nervous system and heart.
Iron is vital to the nervous system and plays an important part in the formation of red blood corpuscles.
Dietary fibres are an essential aid to digestion.

Economy size – NET 600g

This pack contains 15 servings of 40 grams.

Made in Scotland

Find the right balance between food and exercise.

Most children are on the go the whole time, and burn up exactly the same amount of energy as they take in as food. But from the age of seven, most of us become less physically active – this means that our automatic appetite control no longer works properly.

A well-balanced diet, where the food you eat matches the energy you use, will help to eliminate the risks of developing a large number of diseases.

What is a kilojoule?
The food we eat is converted by the body into energy. Energy used to be measured in **calories**, but nowadays it is measured in **joules**. 1 joule is the energy needed to raise 1 kilo ten centimetres. 1 kilojoule (kJ) = 1,000 joules.

Exercise can help you burn up more than ten times as much energy.
If you lie still all day long, you use about 100kJ for every kilo you weigh. If you run all day, you burn up about 1,000kJ for every kilo. If you weigh 72 kilos, this means 7,200kJ if you lie still, and 72,000kJ if you run all day long.

When you stand, you use twice as much energy as when you are lying down. When you walk, you use 5 times as much energy.

HEALTHIBREK

Tastes good and does you good!

Turn over for Activities

CHECKPOINT BOOKS

Titles in the series

101 KEEP-WARM IDEAS

by Ann Lamacraft

Contents

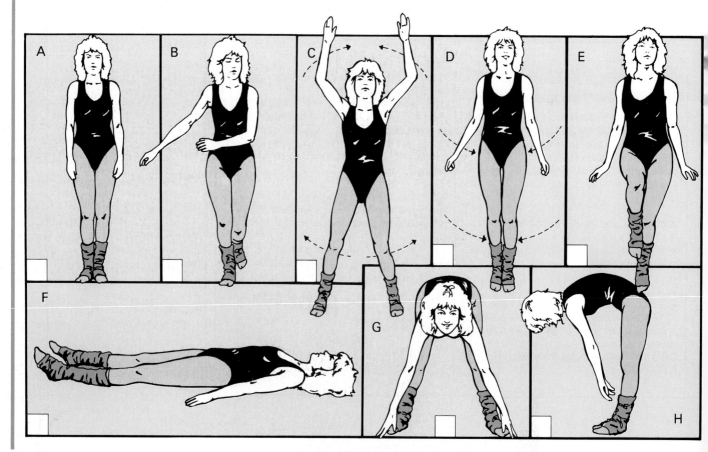

ACTIVITIES

A Healthibrek

1 **Pair work**   Tick the statements that are true, according to the information on the Healthibrek packet on page 143. Give your reasons.

a Eating Healthibrek will
  A improve your sense of balance. ☐
  B help you to lose weight. ☐
  C make it easier for your body to digest food. ☐
  D make you less likely to become ill. ☐
  E make you feel younger. ☐
  F allow you to run all day long. ☐
  G give you at least a quarter of all the vitamins you need. ☐

b Look at the statements again. Which ones are true about taking exercise?

c Most young children
  A automatically eat the right amount of food. ☐
  B are more active than adults. ☐
  C run everywhere all the time. ☐

d Healthibrek is most suitable for
  A children under seven. ☐
  B adults. ☐
  C children over six. ☐
  D adults and children over six. ☐

2 Use your own words to explain what a kilojoule is.

3 What do you think the main purpose of the information is?
  a to educate the public
  b to say that Healthibrek is healthy
  c to say that Healthibrek tastes good

4 Find expressions in the text that match these definitions:
  a active, working without rest
  b get rid of
  c portion of food
  d network of nerves in the body
  e relating to food value
  f desire for food
  g transformed, changed from one form to another
  h process within the body of changing food so that it can be used by the body

5 **Discussion** Is it important to know what the food you eat contains? What are the regulations about labelling food in your country? Would a packet like the Healthibrek packet persuade you to buy this cereal?

6 **Debate** 'It's better to be happy and fat than miserable and thin.'

7 **Group work**. Choose a food item not normally thought of as healthy (for instance hamburgers or potato crisps) and compose all the information needed for the packet or wrapper. Think up a way of emphasising its healthier aspects, presenting it in such a way that people who are concerned about nutrition will want to buy it.

B Books

1 Which books in the Checkpoint series would be useful in these situations? Write down the catalogue numbers of the titles.

a You are interested in flowers and plants. _____

b You are overweight. _____

c Your house needs some minor repairs. _____

d You're going to have a party. _____

e You want something to keep your children amused. _____

f You want to know how to deal with illness and accidents. _____

g You want to make yourself look more attractive. _____

h You haven't got much time for cooking. _____

2 Look at the contents list of *101 Keep-Warm Ideas*. Which chapters will give you advice on

a wearing the right clothes?
b keeping warm at night?
c keeping your house warm?
d how old people can keep warm?

3 **Group work**

a Choose one of the Checkpoint titles and make up a Contents list of seven or eight chapter headings.
b Individually, choose one of your chapter headings and write notes about what information and advice would be included under it.
c Imagine that the other members of the group have asked for advice on the topic covered by your chapter. Use your notes to help you give the advice.

4 **Exam practice**   In 120–180 words, write down exactly what you would say if asked by your fellow students for this advice.

C Listening: 'Keep Warm'

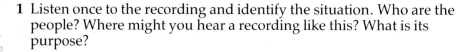

1 Listen once to the recording and identify the situation. Who are the people? Where might you hear a recording like this? What is its purpose?

2 Look at the illustrations on page 144, and listen to the recording as many times as you need to. Write numbers in the boxes in the illustrations to show the order in which the positions are described. Some illustrations are not needed: when you are quite sure that a particular position is not described, mark the box with a cross.

3 In pairs, practise giving the instructions for the 'Keep Warm' exercises.

4 **Discussion**   Would you enjoy doing the exercises described here? Is it important to keep your body in trim? What sort of exercise do you do, and why do you do it?

5 **Pair work**   Think up some more advice for the 'Keep Warm' programme. Imagine that one of you is Dr Henderson and the other is the programme presenter. Act out the rest of the programme in front of the class.

UNIT 11 HEALTH AND FIRST AID

LANGUAGE STUDY

Vocabulary

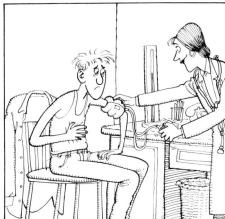

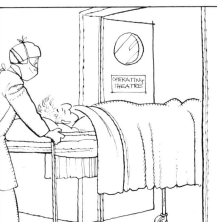

Word families:
sickness and health

A Look at the picture story and fill in the spaces below with the correct form of words from the list.
For example:

examine: **examination**

If you do not know the other forms of the words, use your dictionary to find them out.

check, cure, diagnose, examine, heal, operate, test, treat

Simon woke up one morning with a terrible pain in his side. He was rushed to hospital, where a doctor _____ (1) him. She _____ (2) his blood pressure and pulse and carried out a number of other _____ (3) before she _____ (4) appendicitis. He asked if it could be _____ (5) with drugs, but she recommended immediate surgery. The surgeon confirmed her _____ (6) and agreed to _____ (7). After the _____ (8), his wound was slow to _____ (9) and he had to have further _____ (10). Finally, he was completely _____ (11), and could lead a normal life again, but he had to see his doctor for a _____ -up (12) after six months.

B Now think about the differences between these pairs of verbs:

cure/heal   test/examine   treat/operate   check/test
diagnose/examine   check/examine   treat/cure

Which word means each of the following?

1 to say what is wrong   _____
2 to make someone better   _____
3 to try to make someone better   _____
4 to get better (for a wound)   _____
5 to look at carefully   _____
6 to see if something is right   _____
7 to carry out an experiment   _____
8 to perform surgery   _____

Have you had any medical experiences similar to Simon's? Tell your story to the rest of the class.

Phrasal verbs: *turn*

C Fill in the spaces using these words:

down, into, off, on, out, over, up

Some words must be used more than once.

1 He was so ill that he couldn't even turn _____ in bed.
2 The director was rushed to hospital with a suspected heart attack but it turned _____ to be indigestion.
3 I was offered a job overseas, but I turned it _____ on health grounds.
4 Turn that radio _____! You'll damage your ears.
5 Turn the oven _____ a bit, or the dinner will never be ready.
6 I was amazed by the number of old friends who turned _____ to visit me when I was in hospital.
7 It's a good idea to turn _____ the water before you go on holiday.
8 Turn the television _____, please. There's a good film starting any minute.
9 If you eat any more bananas, you'll turn _____ one!
10 I lost my teddy bear years ago, but it turned _____ last week when we moved house.

Now write your own sentences using the phrasal verbs with *turn*.

Verbs easily confused: *lie* and *lay*

D Fill in the spaces:

Infinitive	Past simple	Past participle
lie	_____	_____
_____	laid	_____

Note: lie/lying, lay/laying

Look at the following examples and complete the definitions.

Lie down and have a rest.
The nurses laid out all the equipment before the operation.

_____ means 'put in a lying position'.
_____ means 'be in a lying position'.

E Put the correct form of *lie* or *lay* in the spaces.

1 How many eggs does the average hen _____ every day?
2 He's been _____ in the same place for hours. Maybe there's something wrong.
3 Has anybody _____ the table yet? It's time to eat.
4 The baby _____ in an incubator for the first four weeks of its life.
5 The surgeon _____ down his tools. The day's work was over.

Verb review: future continuous, future perfect and future perfect continuous

A Complete the gaps below.

+	−	?
Future continuous		
I will be doing.	She _____	_____ you _____?

This tense is used to express actions or states that begin before and continue up to (or after) a given time in the future.

	Future perfect simple	
They _____	He will not have done.	_____ you _____?

This tense is used to express actions or events completed before a given time in the future.

	Future perfect continuous	
I will have been doing.	We _____	_____ you _____ _____?

The use of this tense resembles that of the present perfect continuous but the given point of time is in the future not the present. Like the present perfect continuous it is most commonly used with *for* or *since*. Compare these examples:

He has been waiting for two hours. (up to now = present perfect continuous)
By six o'clock he will have been waiting for five hours. (up to a future time = future perfect continuous
By seven o'clock he will have gone. (action completed before a future time = future perfect simple)

B Charlie has just received this postcard from an American friend, who would like to come and stay with him.

Jan 3, 1988

Dear Charlie,
I hope you are well. May I come and visit you for a couple of weeks? I could come mid-February, mid-March, or any time between April and November.
I sure would love to see you again.
Write soon,
Yours, Bill

Mr C
275
CH
H
E

YEAR PLANNER

JAN	
FEB	27th Report due (10,000 words)
MAR	1-21 Teaching on residential course
APR	15th Baby due
MAY	
JUN	Mum here for hip operation
JUL	
AUG	Mum still here, Convalescing
SEP	To Greece with Mary + Baby Robert + Jamie to Mother-in-Law
OCT	
NOV	
DEC	

The problem is that Charlie's year looks very busy.

Charlie's advice to his American friend is:

Don't come in mid-February. I'll be spending every evening in my study.

Complete these other sentences for him.

1 Don't come in March. _____ during the week and _____ _____ at weekends.
2 Don't come in early April. _____ ready for the baby.
3 Don't come at the end of April. _____ the children.
4 _____ very little sleep.
5 _____ my mother.
6 _____ in our house.
7 _____ on the beach in Greece.

C   As you can see from the picture opposite, Charlie feels that his problems will be over by the end of the year. So he writes to his American friend:

Come in November. My report will have been published by then.
I will have been resting for a month . . .

Continue his letter by expanding the cues into complete sentences.

1 November/baby/start/sleep/night.
2 Mother/have/operation.
3 Hope/she/complete recovery.
4 November/preparation/next residential course/not/start.
5 Wife/not/go/back/work/yet.
6 Hope/my blood pressure/return/normal.
7 By then/sleep/properly/a while.
8 Children/stay/mother-in-law/month.
9 I/have/long holiday.
10 I/not/worry/work/month.

D Imagine that a friend from many thousands of miles away has written to you asking when he/she can come to stay with you for a month or so. Write back saying which times of the year are convenient and which are not and why.

Grammar revision: articles

What do these sentences tell you about when 'the' is used and not used?

Susan would like to learn to play the violin.
The Welsh are very keen that their language should not die.*
Education for the disabled is improving all the time.
That's the third time my operation has been cancelled.
It's now possible to cross the Atlantic in only three hours.
Can I speak to the person in charge?
The Niger is a major communications route in West Africa.
The Soviet Union, the United States and France are all popular holiday destinations.
They had two cars for sale: a Ford and a Fiat. I chose the Fiat.
The first of January is New Year's Day.

*We say: *the Welsh, the Irish, the British, the English, the Spanish, the French, the Dutch, the Swiss.* We also use *the* with nationalities ending in *-ese: the Vietnamese.* But with other nationalities a plural form is used: *(the) Scots, (the) Italians,* etc.

A Now put *a*, *an* or *the* in the following sentences where necessary.

1 Mauritius is _____ island in _____ Indian Ocean.
2 He is working on _____ new hearing aid for _____ deaf.
3 _____Rhine flows through _____ Germany.
4 _____ twenty-fourth of December is _____ Christmas Eve.'
5 _____ pianos are very difficult to move.
6 The doctor is seeing _____ patient. I think it's _____ last one.
7 _____ Americans have to take out private medical insurance.
8 I spoke to _____ man that Nurse Jones was complaining about.
9 We keep two dogs in the laboratory. This one is _____ labrador and that is _____ husky. _____ labrador is friendly but don't go near _____ husky.

Look at these sentences with no article.

In some countries murder is punishable by death.
Life is very hard in countries at war.
Oxford Street is extremely crowded just before Christmas.
She's studying medicine at university.

Compare them with:

The war in Afghanistan has been going on for many years.
The life of a butterfly is very short.
The street was so crowded, I couldn't get into the supermarket.
She's a secretary at the university.

B Now complete the sentences:

1 The death _____.
2 _____ at the school.
3 Work _____.
4 The work _____.
5 Women _____.
6 The men _____.
7 The life _____.
8 The prison _____.
9 The war _____.
10 The medicine _____.
11 Science _____.
12 _____ in prison.

C Now complete this summary of a few basic rules for using articles. Write *the*, *a*, or *no article* in the spaces.

_____ is used the first time something is mentioned.
_____ is used to refer to something already mentioned.
_____ is used with unique things.
_____ is used with abstracts.
_____ is used with something made unique or precise by additional information (. . . weather *in England*).
_____ is used where there is no plural form for a nationality.

Discuss further rules with your teacher and add them to the summary.

Speech work: consonants (1)

Here are some pairs of consonants that are very similar except that one in each pair is voiced and the other unvoiced:

unvoiced	voiced
/p/	/b/
/f/	/v/
/t/	/d/
/k/	/g/
/s/	/z/

A Practise saying the words in the different sets below and see if your partner can tell which word you are saying.

1 pin/bin
pig/big
cap/cab
peach/beach
pat/bat

2 leaf/leave
off/of
safe/save
few/view
fan/van

3 bit/bid
matter/madder
set/said
tip/dip
seat/seed

4 cold/gold
cot/got
card/guard
back/bag
pick/pig

5 price/prize
sip/zip
Sue/zoo
niece/knees
peace/peas

6 lift/lived
cocks/cogs
locked/logged
raced/raised
roped/robed

Note. It is difficult to know whether a word ending in *-se* is pronounced /s/ or /z/. Make your own lists of words with this ending as you come across them.

B Now read the dialogue below taking particular care over voiced and unvoiced consonants.

Functions: worry, regrets, reassurance

Paul: I'm really worried about catching some terrible disease while we're here. I wish I'd had all the jabs.

Tony: Relax! We're only here for a couple of days and we're being careful about what we eat.

Paul: It was stupid to come unprotected, though.

Tony: Stop worrying! It'll all be all right.

A Find phrases in the dialogue to add to these lists:

Worry	*Regrets*	*Reassurance*
I'm concerned about . . .	I should have . . .	There is no cause for concern.
I'm scared of . . .	Why didn't I . . .	Come on!
I'm afraid of . . .	I regret (+ing) . . .	There's no need to worry.

Which three expressions do you think are the most formal?

B The dialogue above is an informal conversation between friends. Imagine that Paul then spoke to his tour guide. Choose expressions from the lists to change the dialogue to a neutral tone.

C Act out these situations with a partner.

1 A doctor is reassuring a patient who is worried about a lump on his hand.
2 One parent is reassuring the other about the fact that their daughter is in hospital for a minor operation.
3 A nurse is persuading a frightened child to let her give him an injection.

EXAM FOCUS

Paper 5: third part

The last, and usually the longest, part of the interview could consist of any one or more of the following:

1 A general discussion on a subject connected with the photograph and the passage.
2 A role play, either with other students or with the examiner.
3 A task where you are asked to describe something or explain how to do something.
4 A conversation based on a printed sheet that you may be given. (See Unit 12, page 166)

The Activities sections in all the units in this book have been designed to give you practice in this part of the examination.

Dos and don'ts

● Be prepared for anything. The purpose of the exercise is to give you an opportunity to talk, and the examiner will be free to choose from a variety of tasks.

● If you don't understand what you are being asked to do, don't be afraid to ask. You could say:

> *I'm sorry, but would you mind explaining that again?*
> or *I'm sorry, but I don't really understand what you want me to do. Could you explain it again?*

This in itself is a conversation and a useful part of the examination.

● If you don't know much about the subject, don't be afraid to say so.

● The subject will be related to that in the earlier parts of the interview. Try to remember words and expressions that you and the examiner have already used. For example, the examiner may have given you some words to help you with the photograph. If you can now use these words, it will give a good impression.

Work in pairs. Discuss how you could deal with the tasks below. Decide what kind of language you need to use. Ask your teacher to help you if necessary. Then, taking it in turns to be the candidate and the examiner, carry out the tasks. If possible, use a tape recorder to record yourselves and then listen critically.

1 If someone you know had (a) hiccoughs (b) nosebleed, how would you advise him or her?
2 What do you think of alternative ways of treating illness, such as acupuncture, homeopathy, etc.?
3 Describe how you can get medical treatment in your country. Do you have to pay for it?
4 Imagine that you have had a lot of headaches recently and you go to the doctor. Act out the conversation. The examiner will be the doctor.
5 Imagine you have a bad cough and you want to buy some medicine from the chemist's. Act out the conversation. The examiner will be the chemist.

**Composition:
formal speeches**

In the last unit we considered how to write informal speeches. However, you may be required to write a more formal speech either to an individual or a group. In addition to the points made on page 138, remember that your speech will need to have a definite introduction, middle (or development) and conclusion, especially if you are addressing a group of people.

Introduction
Useful openings are:
    Good morning/afternoon/evening, ladies and gentlemen.
    (First of all) I should like to introduce/welcome/thank/present/say . . .
    Let me begin by . . .

Development
This section should give some information about the place, person or event concerned.

Conclusion
This section often repeats the message of the Introduction in different words:
    Once again, I would/should like to . . .
    In conclusion, I would . . .
    To sum up, . . .
    It therefore gives me great pleasure to . . .
And finally, you should thank your listeners.

A   Read this outline speech:

Good afternoon, everybody. I have great pleasure in welcoming Dr
_____, who has kindly agreed to come and talk _____ although
she is _____. _____ has lived and worked in _____ for many
_____ and has also done a great deal of _____. Her book
'_____' gives a very vivid account of her life's work and I'm sure that
after _____ we will all _____.
So, allow me to introduce _____. Thank you.

Now answer these questions:

1 Who do you think the speaker is addressing?
2 What is the purpose of the speech?

In groups of three, fill in the spaces with ideas of your own.

B   In the same groups, write the talk given by the speaker introduced in A.

C   You have been asked to thank the speaker publicly at the end of her speech. Write the exact words you would say in your 'vote of thanks'. Stand up in front of the class and give your speeches.

ACCIDENTS AND FIRST AID

BLEEDING

Bleeding will generally stop if you apply firm pressure, which allows clotting to occur. Mild bleeding can be controlled if treated as a Wound (see page 22). What follows here concerns severe bleeding.

1 **Immediately press hard** on the wound, either pinching together its edges with thumb and finger or using the palm of your hand. Even if your hands are dirty act at once.

2 **Raise a bleeding limb,** maintaining pressure all the time. However, if circumstances suggest a fracture, keep him still.

3 **Get the patient lying down,** unless you think the movement would seriously disturb a fracture.

4 **Slip a thick pad** on to the wound, under your hand or fingers, maintaining pressure all the while. For the pad use anything handy; a handkerchief, towel or scarf will serve.

5 **Bandage the pad, very firmly.** A necktie, towel, belt or stocking can be the bandage. Do not let the pressure go until bandaging is complete.

6 **Apply anti-shock measures** and get medical help or an ambulance.

7 **Keep a watch on the bandage.** If bloodstaining oozes through, then the control has been insufficient. Do *not* remove anything but apply another pad and firm bandaging over the stain. Move the injured part as little as possible, so as not to disturb clotting.
See also Ear Bleeding (page 12); Nose Bleeding (page 20), and Tooth Socket Bleeding (page 21).

TOOTHACHE

Aspirin or paracetamol and an early dental appointment are the main actions. But oil of cloves applied to the tooth (not on the gum and not repeatedly) can be temporarily helpful while waiting for treatment.

TOOTH SOCKET BLEEDING

The socket may bleed heavily some hours after a dental extraction. Do not plug the socket itself but let the patient bite hard on a thick gauze pad (or handkerchief) placed over the area. He should maintain this pressure for at least 15 minutes. It will be easier for him if he sits, with his elbow on a table and a hand cupped under the chin to give counter-pressure.

UNCONSCIOUSNESS

In first aid the cause of the person's unconsciousness is less important than the fact that he may choke and die if left on his back with his head bent forward. Blood, saliva or vomit could then flow back into the air tube. Also the tongue, floppy in the patient's unconscious state, can fall back and block the throat.
In all cases:

1 Check whether the victim has stopped breathing and needs artificial respiration (see page 2).

2 If he is breathing but with obvious difficulty in getting air in and out, quickly sweep his mouth with your finger to get out any obstruction, including dentures, then gently and smoothly bend his head well back and keep it thus; this will move the tongue clear of the throat. (Do not twist the head at the neck; see the note on fractured spine on page 17.)

3 Once you are satisfied about the breathing make sure there is no point of severe bleeding to be controlled. Also quickly cover any wounds.

4 Now you have to turn him into the Recovery Position, but first do your best to check any likelihood of a fracture. This should be protected against

FAINTING

If the victim merely feels faint let him lie down. Loosen any tight clothes (collar, braces, belt), raise his legs a little with cushions or folded blankets beneath them. Cover him loosely. Tell him to take deep slow breaths. He is likely to recover soon, and is just as likely to want to get up again before he is fully better. Keep him comfortably lying down a little longer, and give him a drink of water.
Someone feeling faint under circumstances where he cannot lie down (e.g. in a theatre auditorium) should bend forward to get his head as low as possible between his knees.
For Unconsciousness, see page 21.

NOSE BLEEDING

The vessel which bleeds is almost always within the soft part of the nose. Grasp the whole lower half of the nose between finger and thumb and maintain pressure for at least 10 minutes. Repeat if necessary. The patient can hold his own nose, and he should sit up, preferably with his elbow resting on a table. He must not blow his nose or sniff.

Nose bleeding after a blow to the head may be more serious. See Head Injury (page 18).

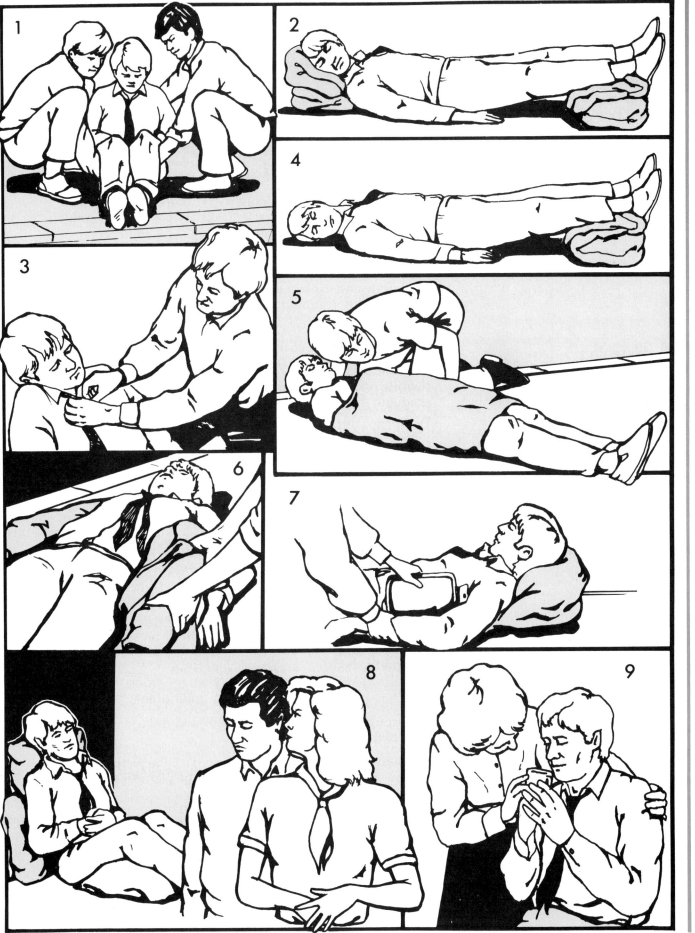

ACTIVITIES

A Accidents and First Aid

1 Discuss in pairs what you would do if you came across a stranger who had had an accident. Would you be able to give First Aid if he or she was suffering from:

a deep cut in the wrist? a nosebleed?
poisoning? a fractured jaw?
loss of consciousness? difficulties with breathing?

2 Look quickly at page 156 to see which of the above conditions are dealt with there. Tick the ones that are.

3 Skim through the text on page 156 to find out for which conditions the following would be useful. Not all of them are useful.

aspirin a cushion oil of cloves
a blanket dentures a handkerchief
a cup a towel water

4 Choose any one of the conditions described in the text to study in detail. Find out exactly what all the words mean, and then demonstrate and explain in your own words to the rest of the class how the condition should be treated.

B Listening: treating shock

1 Listen to the first part of the recording and write in the missing words.

In medical terms, shock is not just _____ (1) upset. It is a very definite physical condition in which the heart and the _____ (2) gradually lose power. Gradually the _____ (3) becomes pale and cold, _____ (4), and perhaps he or she even loses _____ (5). Shock can result from all _____ (6) injuries – bleeding, wounds, burns and _____ (7) – and the speed of the patient's _____ (8) depends on the _____ (9) of the damage. So, whenever someone has been badly injured, you must do two things: you must give _____ (10) help for the actual injury itself, and you must also do something to _____ (11) or at least to try and reduce the shock process. Now, here are one or two _____ (12) on how to do this.

2 Which of the words you have written in Exercise 1 match these definitions?
   a broken bones _____ f person who is
   b feeling sleepy _____ suffering _____
   c getting worse _____ g relating to a particular
   d important, serious _____ thing _____
   e movement of the blood h seriousness _____
   around the body _____ i stop _____
   j suggestions,
   indications _____

3 Look through the pictures on page 157 and discuss what is happening in each of them.

4 Now listen to the rest of the recording. Tick the pictures that show what you *should* do, and put crosses by the pictures that show what you *shouldn't* do.

5 Listen to the second part of the recording again (from 'First of all, you mustn't move . . .'). A number of reasons are given for the various pieces of advice. Write notes saying what these reasons are and which pictures they relate to, like this:

Picture 4. Reason: To help the blood flow to the heart, lungs and brain.

6 Using your notes and the pictures, give a talk on how to treat shock.

7 In pairs or groups discuss the subject of First Aid. Use the following questions to get you started.

● How important is it to be able to give First Aid? Have you ever been in a situation where you were required to give First Aid?
● Which First Aid techniques are most important for *everybody* to learn?

C Group work: health headlines

1 ● The class should divide into four or five groups, each responsible for four or five of the headlines below.
● Make sure you understand your headlines – consult a dictionary or your teacher if necessary. Discuss the stories that might lie behind them, and decide which of them represents the most serious problem to mankind.
● Report back to the rest of the class. Explain the meaning of your headlines, and say which you have chosen as the most serious problem, and why.
● Imagine that your group is the Government Health and Safety Committee, set up to decide how £10 million is to be spent on improving the situation in your country. How will you spend the money? Make a list of the areas which you think should be given priority (e.g. fighting AIDS, cancer research, improving road safety) together with the amount of money you would like to allocate to each.
● Tell the rest of the class about your decisions and your reasons for making them. Compare your list with those produced by the other groups.

2 **Written work** You have been asked to advise the Government Health and Safety Committee which *one* area of public health should be given most money. Write exactly what you would say to the committee. Use between 120 and 180 words.

Alcohol deaths increase

Mentally handicapped girl should be sterilized, says judge

AIDS result of biological warfare experiment, says top scientist

Euthanasia doctor acquitted

The price of human health: thousands of animals tortured to death

"Passive" smoking: link with cancer

CHILDREN SUFFER AS DENTISTS' FEES RISE

13 die in motorway blaze

Pope stands firm on birth control

Prescription charges up 500% in last three years

Headache tablets did not cause blindness, drugs firm claims

Boy contracts rabies after visit to India

12,000 feared dead in earthquake

Girl on health diet dies of starvation

Genetic engineering produces "better" sheep

DEAF GROUPS LOBBY FOR SIGN LESSONS

HOSPITAL CLOSED AFTER COCKROACHES FOUND IN KITCHEN

Cancer risk at nuclear plant

Human brain transplant now possible

UNIT **12** LEARNING

LANGUAGE STUDY

Vocabulary

Word families:
people in education

Look at these two groups of words and discuss what the differences in use are within each group. In what sort of places would you find these people?

student	teacher
pupil	tutor
trainee	trainer
apprentice	instructor
learner	professor
	coach

A Choose the correct words. In some cases more than one may be possible.

The man driving the car in the picture above is a (1) *pupil/learner/ student*. His (2) *teacher/trainer/instructor* is finding him very hard to teach. She is new to the job and her own (3) *trainer/professor/coach* had not prepared her for anything like this. She wishes she had stuck to

160

her old job as an Olympic swimming (4) *trainer/coach/tutor*. However, she is not suffering as much as her companion, who is extremely embarrassed. The children on the pavement are (5) *students/pupils/learners* at the local primary school where he is a(n) (6) *student/apprentice/trainee* teacher. As his (7) *tutor/instructor/professor* from the college is coming to the school tomorrow he will have to think of something fast to regain the respect of the children. The answer – a story about his twin brother and his efforts to learn to drive!

Tell the rest of the class about your experiences when learning a new skill or subject.

Phrasal verbs: *bring*

B Look at the examples of phrasal verbs with *bring* and choose a definition for each one from the list below.

Examples
1 As his parents had died, the boy was *brought up* by his grandparents.
2 Let's not *bring up* the subject of your learning to fly just yet. It will only worry him.
3 It seems strange that any reminder of his years as a driving instructor *brings on* one of his headaches.
4 After the child had been unconscious for several days, they decided to play his favourite music in an attempt to *bring* him *round*.
5 How are we going to *bring* his father *round* to the idea that Joe will not be wasting his time at art school?
6 They are *bringing out* a new book on local education soon.
7 They are *bringing in* a new method of assessment next year.
8 Jim wanted his holiday to be *brought forward* to fit in with the school terms.

Definitions

a cause
b persuade
c rear
d make earlier

e restore to consciousness
f start to talk about something
g manufacture or publish
h introduce something new

Write your own sentences using these phrasal verbs.

Verbs easily confused:

C Choose the verb that best completes each sentence.

1 Will you _____ me how to make that sound?
   A train   **B** practise   **C** learn   **D** teach

2 You will need a pencil and paper to _____ this problem. It is too hard to do in your head.
   A find out   **B** discover   **C** realise   **D** work out

3 He was a difficult pupil: he wouldn't let any of the teachers _____ him.
   A understand   **B** know   **C** get to know   **D** find out

4 If you want to play the piano well, you must _____ every day.
   A train   **B** practise   **C** revise   **D** learn

5 As every pupil knows, Columbus _____ America in 1492.
   A got to know   **B** found out   **C** discovered   **D** knew

D The alternatives above consist of twelve other verbs connected with the subject of learning. Write twelve sentences of your own to show the differences in meaning of these verbs.

**Verb review:
reported speech (2)**

advise, agree, ask, command, order, promise, refuse, tell, threaten

A   Sort the above words into two groups:

Group A – verbs which lead to action from the listener
Group B – verbs which lead to action or non-action from the speaker

Which group of verbs fits into each of the following patterns?

1 To _____ someone (not) to do something. □
2 To _____ (not) to do something. □

B   Using verbs from the list, rewrite the sentences without direct speech. For example:

'Sit down!' she said.
She ordered us to sit down.

1 'I wouldn't leave school yet if I were you,' said his father.
2 'I'll help you, don't worry,' said their teacher.
3 'I'm not going out with that customer,' said the driving instructor.
4 'Practise that movement every day while you are warming up,' said the coach.
5 'Children, if you don't behave, I'll keep you behind after school,' said the teacher.
6 'Fine. We'll start training tomorrow,' said the instructor.
7 'Would you please help me with my homework?' said the student to his neighbour.
8 'Men! Finish that work immediately!' said the officer.

Say, suggest, explain

To the list of verbs commonly used in reported speech we can add *say, suggest,* and *explain*. The structures that follow some of the verbs may not always follow other verbs.

C   For each verb, write in the box the numbers of the sentences that it could be used in. The first has been done for you.

advised	1, 5	*agreed*	
explained		*ordered*	
said		*suggested*	
asked		*commanded*	
promised		*refused*	
told		*threatened*	

1 She _____ me to do it.
2 She _____ why they did it.
3 She _____ doing it immediately.
4 She _____ to do it.
5 She _____ me.
6 She _____ it to me.
7 She _____ me why they did it.

D   Write twelve sentences of your own, each containing one of the verbs in the list. Use the sentences above as guides but replace *do* and *it* by other words or phrases.

Sometimes in reported speech it is not necessary to repeat any of the original words. For example, *I'm sorry* can be reported as *He apologised*.

E Match the statements below with the verbs on the right.

Hi!	agree
No, I won't.	blame
I'm very grateful.	criticise
Well done!	disagree
Here you are.	give
I'm very sorry to hear that.	greet
You didn't do that very well!	praise
It's your fault.	refuse
You're right.	sympathise
No, it isn't.	thank

Can you think of any more verbs like this?

F Write the story in the past tense without using direct speech, as if you were the instructor.

Grammar revision:
It's time, I wish, I'd rather

A Look at sentences 1–10 and match them with ideas a–e in the table below. Look at which verb forms aer used for each idea and complete the second column. Choose the verb forms from the list below the table.

1 I wish I had stayed at school an extra year.
2 I wish you wouldn't interrupt me all the time.
3 I wish she lived a bit nearer.
4 I wish they hadn't told my parents.
5 I wish I spoke fluent English.
6 I wish we were lying on a hot, sunny beach.
7 It's time we did some work.
8 It's time for me to go.
9 I'd rather you didn't help me.
10 I'd rather do it myself.

	Sentence numbers	Verb forms
a I regret something in the past.		*I wish* + _____
b I want someone to do (or stop doing) something.		*I wish* + _____
c It's a shame that something is (or is not) true.		*I wish* + _____
		or + _____
d I think something should be done now.		*It's time* + _____
		or + _____
e I'd prefer something to happen (or not happen).		*I'd rather* + _____
		or + _____

Verb forms: past simple, past continuous, past perfect, *would* + infinitive, infinitive, infinitive with *to*.

B   Look at the picture at the beginning of this unit. Make sentences about how the people feel, by using the structures in Exercise 1 to expand these cues.

1 He/wish/learn/younger.
2 He/wish/children/go/away.
3 He/wish/stay/home.
4 He/wish/learn/different town.
5 He/wish/able/drive.
6 He/rather/be/home.
7 Time/lesson/finish.
8 Instructor/wish/home.
9 Instructor/rather/she/not/have/another/lesson.
10 Time/instructor/find/new job.

Using these structures write sentences to say how you feel about:

a your schooling.
b the way you are learning English now.
c your career.

Speech work: consonants (2)

Below is a list of further consonants that can cause pronunciation difficulties. Only some will be difficult for you and those will depend on your mother tongue. Mark the consonants that you think present problems for speakers of your language. Then try to think of more pairs or groups of words that differ only in the one consonant sound.

/l/r/	alive/arrive	/b/v/	ban/van
/j/dʒ/tʃ/ʃ/	your/jaw/chore/shore	/w/g/	wood/good
/θ/t/s/d/	thank/tank/sank/dank	/w/v/f/	wine/vine/fine
/ð/d/z/	breathe/breed/breeze	/h/	harm/arm

Read the dialogue below with a partner; if possible, record yourselves on a tape recorder. Help each other to decide which consonants are causing most problems. Then read it again, concentrating on those particular sounds.

Functions: checking understanding

Mr Beckett: I think that, all things considered, the best course of action for you would be to go out and get a job. Is that clear?
Tom: Are you saying that I should not stay on and do research?
Mr Beckett: Yes, I suppose I am.
Tom: Does that mean that you would not give me a good reference if I applied for a research grant?
Mr Beckett: Don't misunderstand me. I am simply giving you advice. I would always support you in whatever you chose to do.

What do you think the relationship is between these two people? How does the style show this?

A   Find phrases from the dialogue to add to these lists. Then practise reading the dialogue aloud, substituting alternative phrases.

Checking your own understanding	*Checking other people's understanding*
If I have understood you correctly . . .	Do you see what I mean?
(Do) you mean . . .	Does that make sense?
In other words . . .	Am I making myself clear?
	Are you with me?

B   Think of something that you know how to make. Explain to your partner how to do it. Keep checking his/her understanding. Your partner should interrupt if he/she is not sure about something.

EXAM FOCUS

Paper 5: third part (2)

Dos and don'ts

In the last part of the interview you may be given something to read. It may be an advertisement, or an information sheet. It may consist of both words and pictures.

● Don't read it in detail. Just get a general idea of what it is about. It is not a comprehension exercise. The purpose is only to provide something to talk about.

● If you don't understand something that you think is important – ask. Otherwise you may not be able to carry on with the conversation.

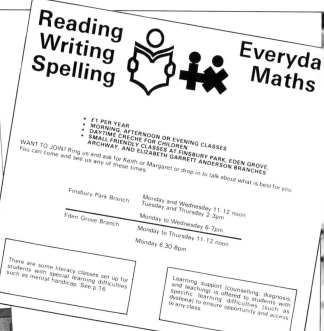

Reading
Writing
Spelling   Everyda
                              Maths

* £1 PER YEAR
* MORNING, AFTERNOON OR EVENING CLASSES
* DAYTIME CRECHE FOR CHILDREN
* SMALL FRIENDLY CLASSES AT FINSBURY PARK, EDEN GROVE, ARCHWAY, AND ELIZABETH GARRETT ANDERSON BRANCHES

WANT TO JOIN? Ring us and ask for Keith or Margaret or drop in to talk about what is best for you. You can come and see us any of these times:

Finsbury Park Branch — Monday and Wednesday 11-12 noon / Tuesday and Thursday 2-3pm

Eden Grove Branch — Monday to Wednesday 6-7pm / Monday to Thursday 11-12 noon / Monday 6.30-8pm

There are some literacy classes set up for students with special learning difficulties such as mental handicap. See p.16

Learning support (counselling, diagnosis, and teaching) is offered to students with specific learning difficulties (such as dyslexia) to ensure opportunity and access to any class.

THE FACTS:

Over 80% of all schools in the U.K. use a BBC micro.

There are over 2000 educational software titles that can be used on BBC micros.

Every BBC micro produced since 1981 may be linked into ECONET, one of the fastest and most flexible networking systems.

Since Acorn introduced the BBC Master Series computers in the Spring of 1986, over 75,000 have been sold.

THE CONCLUSION:

Build on your investment. The BBC Master Compact will give you an entry into the widely acclaimed Master Series technology.

A highly flexible tool, the Compact can handle computer assisted learning as well as school administration now and into the foreseeable future. With disc drive, monitor and software packages included, the Compact represents the most economical computer system a school can buy.

Call Jeremy Preston on 0223 214411. He'll give you all the facts.

 The BBC Master Compact.
A Master Series Computer from Acorn.

 Acorn
The choice of experience

A   Look at the printed extract. Then answer the questions.

1 What do you think it is?
2 Why would people go to these classes?
3 Why do you think they are necessary?
4 If people in your country have difficulty with reading or writing, what can they do?

B   Look at the second extract. Then answer the questions.

1 What questions do you think the examiner might ask about this?
2 What discussion topics do you think it could lead to?

Composition: revision

A   Look at these titles and say what kind of composition each one is asking for and what style of writing it needs.

1 My first day at school.
2 A new student has just joined your class. He has asked you to explain about the school and the classes. Write what you would say to him/her.
3 Do you think it is better for boys and girls to go to separate schools? Why?
4 'At last I understood why my father had not helped me.' Write a story ending with these words.
5 You want to give up a course you are attending. Write a letter to your parents to tell them this and explain why.

B   Choose two of the above titles. Look back at the sections in this book that cover the types of composition you have chosen, and write the compositions under exam conditions.

Checking

It is very important that you do not make unnecessary, careless mistakes in your compositions. They will give a very bad impression and considerably reduce your marks.

Look back over the compositions you have written during the course. Make a note of the mistakes you seem to make most, for example: past tenses, articles, prepositions, punctuation, spelling.

Why do you think you make these mistakes? Is it because:

a you have not understood something?
b you are influenced by your first language?
c you are being too ambitious?

Discuss these points individually with your teacher.

C   Choose the three most important categories of mistakes that you make and that you can correct yourself.

1 _____
2 _____
3 _____

Now look at the compositions that you have just written. Read them through three times: the first time, look only for mistakes in the first category; the second time, mistakes in the second category; and the third time, mistakes in the third category. Be careful not to change what is already correct!

Hand your work to a neighbour and ask him/her to check again, looking for the same points.

Illiteracy is up to 7 million, team finds

By Edward Vulliamy

At least seven million people in Britain are illiterate, according to research by a team at Lancaster University transmitted on Granada's World in Action programme last night.

This figure – which challenges the previous estimate of two million – is reflected in the results of a World in Action poll conducted by MORI in Rochdale among 500 adults and 500 school-leavers, who took a literacy test.

The results show that 52 per cent of teenagers and 44 per cent of adults could not understand the instructions on a fire notice, and 44 per cent of teenagers and adults could not understand a basic timetable.

In elementary maths, 18 per cent of teenagers and 13 per cent of adults had problems, and 10 per cent of teenagers and 7 per cent of adults had problems with basic reading tests.

Asked what number was 50 per cent of 180, 32 per cent of teenagers and 28 per cent of adults could not answer, and 25 per cent of teenagers and 26 per cent of adults could not fill in a simple job application form.

The Lancaster project's director, Dr Mary Hamilton, says that up to 13 per cent of British people could be validly classed as illiterate.

Her research is based on an analysis of the National Children's Development Study, which monitored the progress of every child born in the first week of March 1958. Her findings involve factors of upbringing which make them as valid for the wealthy south as for the poorer north, she said.

On the film the personnel director of the North-west Cooperative Society, Mr Alan Gill, said that more than half of the 300 job applicants who wrote to him each year had trouble spelling their own name or address or the address of their school. They would be unlikely to get interviews, he said.

The programme researcher, Ms Diane Nelmes, said: "It was only when a lot of people who would formerly have automatically gone into manual work started to show up on training courses that the extent of the problem revealed itself."

from: Delfina del Mata

I would like to have an intensive two-week course during March as I shall be taking part in an International Trade Conference in April. I think it would be best for me to have personal tuition for five or six hours a day, and to live with an English-speaking family.

from: Jean-Paul Droger

I intend to take the Cambridge Proficiency examination soon, and so I should like to spend two months in the London area during the summer, with about three hours tuition every day. In my spare time I need to be given the opportunity to meet as many English people as possible.

from: Gunhild Ekstrand

I teach English at a middle-school in Sweden, and I am arranging a trip for ten of my pupils to visit England for two weeks during the summer. They are all 12 years old, and would like to spend half the time in the classroom, and the rest of the time with organized social activities and excursions.

CLASSIFIED ADVERTISEMENTS

Sels College London
64-65 Long Acre, Covent Garden, London WC2E 9JH Tel. 01-240-2581, Tlx. 268312 WESCOM SELSCOL

Sels College, recognised by the British Council, is one of the leading schools of English in London open throughout the year. It is situated near the Royal Opera House in Covent Garden, one of the most historic and interesting parts of London. There are courses for beginners and advanced students. Students, aged 16 to 60, study in small groups of 5 to 9 or take individual lessons.

International House – Northumbria,
24, Northumberland Road, Newcastle-upon-Tyne, NE1 8JZ. Tel: 091-2329551.

Small, friendly school in an interesting part of the North of England. General English courses from beginners to advanced level. Examinations classes. Special Executive courses for professional and business users of English. Summer holiday courses with full social programme and excursions include Edinburgh and the Lake District. Write for details.

The Brighton and Hove School of English
7-9 Wilbury Villas, Hove, E. Sussex, BN3 6GB Tel: 0273 738182 Telex Englang 87323 FSI-G.

General courses in preparation for Cambridge First Certificate & Proficiency examinations. Summer Holiday Courses. Intensive Courses. Friendly school in residential area. Host-family accommodation.

English Immersion Courses (Keith & Ruth Carr),
59 Belmont Road, Portswood, Southampton, SO2 1GD. Tel: Southampton (0703) 551920.

One or two adult students live in their teacher's home for up to three weeks, receiving 15-20 hours one-to-one teaching per week. Courses tailored to students' business, technical or academic needs.

Anglian School of English,
81/83 Norfolk Road, Cliftonville, Margate, Kent CT9 2HX. Tel: (0843) 293700. Telex: 965536 MARGI EG (Attn Anglian).

Small friendly school, owned by teachers. Open all year, General and Business English. Properly qualified teachers. Small multinational classes. Any length course from two weeks – begin any Monday – 20 or 25 hours per week. Individual students only, aged 16+. Excellent full-board family accommodation

Wimbledon School of English,
41 Worple Road, London, SW19 4JZ Tel: 01-947 1921

Full-time and part-time courses in English leading to Cambridge First Certificate and Proficiency Examinations. Special Summer courses. Pleasant, friendly school situated in a residential area but within easy reach of central London. Accommodation arranged with selected British families.

ACTIVITIES

A Illiteracy

1 Read the newspaper article opposite and find the information needed to complete the table.

		0	10	20	30	40	50	60	70%
cannot understand fire instructions	adults								
	teenagers								
cannot understand timetable	adults								
	teenagers								
	adults	▨							
	teenagers	▨							
	adults	▨							
	teenagers	▨							
cannot give answer to '50% of 180'	adults								
	teenagers								
cannot fill in job application form	adults								
	teenagers								
	adults	▨							
	teenagers								

2 Find words in the article that match these definitions:
  a ability to read and write
  b investigation to discover new facts
  c people who are just leaving school
  d science of numbers
  e survey of public opinion
  f truthfully, with good reason
  g unable to read or write
  h very simple

3 **Pair work** Cover up the article and use the completed table to help you describe the survey's findings to your partner.

4 **Discussion**
  ● Do the statistics surprise you?
  ● What might be the causes that lie behind the statistics?
  ● Do you think a survey in your country would produce similar results?
  ● What do you think are the main problems for people who are illiterate?
  ● Can you think of any solutions?

B Information retrieval: choosing a language school

You work for an agency that helps foreign students of English to find schools and courses in the U.K. that suit their particular needs. Using information from the advertisements opposite, write a report in three paragraphs of about 50 words each recommending suitable schools for the people who have written the letters. Start each paragraph like this:

For Delfina del Mata I recommend . . .
For Jean-Paul Droger I recommend . . .
For Gunhild Ekstrand I recommend . . .

C Listening:
Hard Times

1 Listen to the recording once only, and answer these questions.

   a Where does the scene take place?

   b Who is Mr Gradgrind?

   c Who is Sissy Jupe?

   d Who is Bitzer?

2 Now read through the following statements and decide which ones are true. Then listen to the tape and check your answers.

   a Mr Gradgrind had never seen Sissy Jupe before. ☐

   b Sissy's real name was Cecilia. ☐

   c Sissy answered Mr Gradgrind confidently. ☐

   d Mr Gradgrind didn't approve of the job of horse-riding. ☐

   e Sissy's father's main job was breaking horses in the circus ring. ☐

   f Sissy's father was a veterinary surgeon. ☐

   g Sissy didn't know what a horse was. ☐

   h Bitzer and Sissy sat in the same ray of sunlight. ☐

   i The sun made Sissy look pale. ☐

   j The sun made Bitzer look even paler than he really was. ☐

   k Bitzer knew what sort of teeth horses have. ☐

   l You can tell a horse's age by looking in its mouth. ☐

3 Discussion

● What point is the writer making when he describes the ray of sunlight and its effect on the two children?

● Did Bitzer really know more about horses than Sissy Jupe did? What did Sissy know about them? Why couldn't she answer Mr Gradgrind's question?

● Part of the writer's purpose is to contrast two different types of education – Sissy Jupe's (gained through experience) and Bitzer's (gained through learning facts in the classroom). Which type of education do you think the writer prefers? Which type do you think is more valuable?

● What do you think should be taught in schools that is not taught?

4 Debate

The purpose of education is to ensure that society runs smoothly.

D
Education

Play the game in groups of four or five students. You will need a die, and a counter, or piece of coloured card, for each student.

1 Place all the counters on the START square.

2 In turn, each player throws the die and moves his counter the number of squares shown on the die.

3 If the counter lands on a square with a black mark (●) or star (☆), put a tick in the appropriate place in the box marked "Keep a tally . . ." . This tally is needed if you land on the square marked "END OF SCHOOL REPORT"

4 If the counter lands on one of the larger boxes, obey the instructions.

5 The winner is the player who first reaches or passes the FINISH square.

4

READING COMPREHENSION

Time allowed: **15 minutes**

Choose the best word or phrase to complete each sentence.

1 Which book would you _____ me to read?
  A suggest   B say   C rather   D advise

2 Ice cream is a tasty and easily prepared _____.
  A desert   B plate   C course   D dessert

3 I'm going to the Far East for my holiday, _____ I really can't afford it.
  A whereas   B while   C although   D in spite of

4 I'm afraid our plan just didn't _____ off.
  A come   B get   C bring   D set

5 Can you please _____ that everyone has got a ticket?
  A control   B check   C assure   D know

6 I don't want to go, but there is no way of getting _____ it.
  A from   B off   C out of   D away

7 I _____ to live in a big industrial city.
  A dislike   B wouldn't like   C would rather not
  D suggest

8 I would _____ you didn't leave just at the moment.
  A rather   B like   C ask   D advise

9 'I really don't like the idea.' 'Neither _____ I.'
  A like   B don't   C nor   D do

10 If I _____ the chance, I would have trained to be a doctor.
  A would have had   B would have   C had had
  D have had

11 I'm very concerned _____ my son's health.
  A of   B on   C from   D about

12 It's no good _____ me of getting the figures wrong!
  A accusing   B blaming   C criticising   D scolding

13 In many ways she _____ me of someone I knew at school.
  A remembers   B reminds   C recalls   D resembles

14 It looks _____ it's going to rain.
  A as   B like as   C as if   D if

15 You'd better take a bus. It's _____.
  A far   B distant   C long   D a long way

16 The news of Henry's death came as a terrible _____.
  A hurt   B pain   C shock   D wound

17 In the accident, the front of my car suffered severe _____.
  A damage   B injury   C shock   D wounds

18 She's doing _____ into the spread of Mesopotamian culture.
  A an examination   B a poll   C research   D a survey

19 The chemist will give you the medicine when you give him this _____.
  A description   B prescription   C receipt   D recipe

20 The koala bear's _____ consists almost entirely of eucalyptus leaves and shoots.
   A diet   B digestion   C nourishment   D nutrition

21 It's vital that our children's handwriting should be _____.
   A illiterate   B legible   C legitimate   D literate

22 The festival this year contains a well-_____ programme of classical and modern music.
   A balanced   B formed   C meant   D thought

23 Here's an excellent _____ on how to get rid of those extra pounds.
   A advice   B hint   C information   D tip

24 At the language school, each student is assigned to his or her own _____.
   A director   B professor   C staff   D tutor

25 Your article would have been better if you'd given your own opinion. You really _____ have been so objective.
   A can't   B mustn't   C needn't   D oughtn't

COMPOSITION

Time allowed: 1½ hours

Write two of the following compositions. Each composition should be between 120 and 180 words.

1 A member of your family is in trouble and you have had to go away for a week or two. Write a letter to your English teacher apologising and explaining what has happened.

2 A 19-year-old friend of yours is trying to decide whether to get a job in his father's factory or take up a job offer abroad, and has asked for your advice. Write what you would say to him.

3 Write about: 'The day my friend saved someone's life'.

4 'Many illnesses are caused by the way we lead our lives.' How far is this true? What do you think can be done about it?

USE OF ENGLISH

Time allowed: 1 hour

A   Put *one* word in each of the numbered spaces:

King Arthur is _____ (1) of the most famous kings of England but he may never _____ (2) existed. Many stories are told _____ (3) his life, and the _____ (4) known one tells of the way he became king. It is _____ (5) that he _____ (6) taken away from his father, the King, as a baby in _____ (7) to save him _____ (8) the King's enemies. He was _____ (9) up as an ordinary child. _____ (10) Arthur was still a young man, his father died. Nobody knew he had _____ (11) a son, and the country _____ (12) a new king. One day a huge stone _____ (13) a sword _____ (14) it magically appeared in a churchyard. On the stone were the _____ (15) 'Whoever pulls this sword out of this stone _____ (16) the trueborn King of England.' Many men _____ (17) to pull the sword out, but _____ (18) of them succeeded. A few days _____ (19), Arthur, who was looking _____ (20) a sword for his brother, saw the sword in the stone and simply pulled it out.

B   Finish each of the following sentences in such a way that it means exactly the same as the sentence printed before it.

1   I'm sorry I am so late, he said.
    He apologised _____.

2   It's a pity we didn't buy that fridge when we saw it.
    I wish _____.

3   This is my first trans-Atlantic flight.
    This is the first time _____.

4   Someone should look at your back.
    You should _____.

5   I can't come because I have to look after my neighbour's children.
    If I _____.

6   We should do something about it now.
    It's time we _____.

7   Sarah can swim further than I can.
    I can't swim _____.

8   I haven't been to the dentist for two years.
    It is _____.

9   The food was so badly burned that nobody could eat it.
    The food was too _____.

10 I don't want you to smoke in here.
    I would _____.

C   Put the correct particle in each space.

1 I think I am going to take _____ woodwork. I need some new bookshelves.

2 It's very strange how he takes _____ the father he has never met.

3 I don't understand how he gets _____ with arriving so late every day.

4 If you haven't got an excuse, make one _____!

5 Not enough people can come to the meeting, so we'll put it _____ until next week.

6 I'm sorry I can't offer you any coffee. We've run _____.

7 I promised I would organise the meeting, but I really don't know how to set _____ it.

8 Many people still remember the day the war broke _____.

9 Our plan to frighten them away didn't come _____.

10 I heard a crash and went out to see what was going _____.

D   Write out the following passage in dialogue form, making all the necessary changes.

The teacher congratulated Ann on getting all the answers right. He then asked Joy for her homework. She gave it to him and he thanked her, praising her neat handwriting. Then he asked Bob if he had done his homework. Bob apologised and told him that he hadn't. The teacher exploded! Although Bob promised to do it that night, the teacher criticised his attitude and said that he wasn't working hard enough. But he said he would give him one more chance before he reported him to the Headteacher. Bob thanked him and promised to try harder in future. The teacher dismissed him rather rudely and shouted a final warning as he left the room.

Teacher: Well done, Ann! You got all the answers right. What about you, Joy? Can I have your homework?
Joy: Yes, here you are.
Teacher: _____

TAPESCRIPT

UNIT 1

**The interview
(page 21)**

Interviewer: Right, Sergeant, I think I'm ready to see them now. Would you call the first applicant, Mr . . . Mr Baker.

Sergeant: Yes, sir. Mr Baker.

Interviewer: Ah, Mr Baker, please take a seat.

Mr Baker: Thank you.

Interviewer: Now, why do you want to be a policeman?

Mr Baker: Well . . . I've done quite a few jobs since leaving school and the idea of being a policeman I find really attractive because it's helping the community, it's . . . doing something worthwhile.

Interviewer: Good, fine. Right, let's just have a look at these details you gave us here. Your surname's Baker. What are your first names?

Mr Baker: John Martin.

Interviewer: And your address?

Mr Baker: 17 Northolt Avenue, Barking, Essex.

Interviewer: Right. Your date of birth is the eighth of April . . .

Mr Baker: 1966, yes.

Interviewer: Good . . . Yes . . . Barking . . . British . . . And you're not married?

Mr Baker: No. Good.

Interviewer: No children?

Mr Baker: No.

Interviewer: Just as well. Now then, your height. You *do* know, don't you, that the minimum height requirement for us is five foot eight? You've put five foot seven and a half on your Application Form.

Mr Baker: Yes.

Interviewer: Were you standing up straight, are you quite sure, when you measured yourself?

Mr Baker: Well, I'm pretty sure . . . I mean, I might be half an inch out. I might be a little bit wrong but . . .

Interviewer: Good, well, we'll leave that for the moment. And your weight?

Mr Baker: It's ten stone seven pounds.

Interviewer: Good. Now you said you've got no major illnesses, you've had no operations . . .

Mr Baker: No, I haven't. My eyes are . . . give me a bit of trouble. I'm a little bit short-sighted.

Interviewer: You wear glasses, do you?

Mr Baker: Yes.

Interviewer: And your sight *with* glasses is all right?

Mr Baker: Yes, it's perfect, yes.

Interviewer: Excellent, good. Now then, what about your education?

Mr Baker: Well, I've got five 'O' levels: Maths, English, French, Geography and Spanish.

Interviewer: Good in languages . . . that could be useful. Now, tell me about your other work before you came to us.

Mr Baker: Well, I started off when I left school . . . I . . . I worked for a taxi firm . . . a local taxi firm, and I worked for them for about eight months and then a friend of mine asked me to come and work for him. He was a plasterer and we decorated people's houses.

Interviewer: Did you enjoy that?

Mr Baker: Yes, I did. It's *very* hard work. But then I did some voluntary social work. I helped old people. I did their shopping, washed their windows and things like that and I found that so satisfying that I wanted to do a job . . . I wanted to find a career that could help people in the way that . . . that social work did.

Interviewer: I see.

Mr Baker: I found that really enjoyable.

Interviewer: Good, good, right. So that's quite a lot of experience. You're quite sure that, having had three jobs before, you don't just want this one for a short period as well?

Mr Baker: No, I'm sure.

Interviewer: Good. Right, now tell me about your interests, your hobbies.

Mr Baker: Well, I like sports, football in particular.

Interviewer: You play, do you?

Mr Baker: Yes, I do, yes.

Interviewer: What position?

Mr Baker: Defence.

Interviewer: Oh good. Now then, let's just have a little look at one or two other things. What . . . what do you think you'd feel if you found yourself in perhaps a slightly violent situation and you had to use some sort of weapon?

Mr Baker: Well, I'd actually rather not use any weapon. I don't think it's necessary always. It depends how violent and what the offender is carrying but, if he's unarmed, I'd prefer not to have a weapon myself and just use diplomacy rather than violence.

Interviewer: And you think you might be capable of that, do you?

Mr Baker: Yes, I think I am, yes.

Interviewer: Good, good. And do you think that the role of the police is to make decisions about who's doing wrong and who's guilty and who's not?

Mr Baker: No, that's for the courts to decide. The police just bring the offenders in front of the court. That's their job.

Interviewer: Good, so you don't think you'd find it too frightening to be out on the street, perhaps on your own, at night?

Mr Baker: No, I don't think so.

Interviewer: Now, I . . . I see you go to the cinema quite a lot?

Mr Baker: Yes, I do.

Interviewer: Yes. And you don't think your attitudes to the police are too influenced by the cinema?

Mr Baker: No, no, of course not. No.

Interviewer: Good. Good. Right, well, thank you very much, Mr Baker. If we want to see you again, we'll let you know. We'll be in touch with you anyway, one way or the other. Thanks for coming to see us.

Mr Baker: Thank you, sir.

Interviewer: Good luck. Goodbye.

UNIT 2

**A radio quiz show
(page 33)**

Questioner: Welcome to Family Quiz! Thank you, thank you and good evening. This is the programme that pits husband against wife to find out who's got the brains of the family. So let's get down to it straightaway and give a warm welcome to tonight's contestants, Mr and Mrs Walsh, of Reading. Mr Walsh, your first name is . . . ?

Peter: Peter.

Questioner: And Mrs Walsh?

Jenny: Jenny.

Questioner: Good. Well now Peter and Jenny, I'm sure you know the

	rules. In round one, I'm going to ask you each alternate questions. If you answer a question correctly, you get ten points. If you get an answer wrong, then your other half can have a shot at it for ten points.. All right?
Jenny:	I think so.
Questioner:	Right. Off we go! The topic for round one is British History and here we go with the first question. Jenny, this one's for you.
Jenny:	Oh!
Questioner:	When was the Battle of Hastings?
Jenny:	1066.
Questioner:	Correct! 1066 is right. Ten points for you, Jenny. Now Peter, let's see if you can live up to her. Second question for you, Peter. Which English King broke with the Roman Catholic church?
Peter:	Henry VIII.
Questioner:	Absolutely right! Henry VIII is correct. It's level pegging then as we come to question three. Jenny, how many wives did Henry VIII have?
Jenny:	Seven.
Questioner:	No . . . I'm afraid I can't allow that. Peter, can you do better?
Peter:	Eight?
Questioner:	No, I'm sorry, neither of you scored there. The correct answer was in fact six. Right . . . question four. Peter, this one's for you. Which Roman general invaded England in 55 BC?
Peter:	Erm . . .
Questioner:	Come on, Peter. I'll have to hurry you.
Peter:	Julius Caesar.
Questioner:	Absolutely right, Peter. Julius Caesar . . . another ten points to you. Now question five. Jenny, which famous Englishman was born in 1564?
Jenny:	William Shakespeare.
Questioner:	Absolutely right. OK. Question six. Peter, when did the First World War end?
Peter:	1940 . . .
Questioner:	No, I'm sorry, I think you're thinking of the Second World War. It happens to all of us. Right, Jenny. Can you do better?
Jenny:	Yes, 1918.
Questioner:	Absolutely right, Jenny. You'll have to watch this one, Peter. It's slipping away from you here. Jenny, question seven. When were England and Scotland first joined under one king?
Jenny:	. . . I don't know.
Questioner:	Peter?
Peter:	1603.
Questioner:	Absolutely right. You don't know the name of the king by any chance?
Peter:	James I?
Questioner:	Absolutely right as well. No extra points there I'm afraid. Right . . . the last question of the round, question eight. Peter, which British king or queen ruled the longest?
Peter:	I don't know, Bob.
Questioner:	Jenny?
Jenny:	. . . Queen Elizabeth . . . er . . . Victoria.
Questioner:	I'll allow that. I'll allow that. It is in fact Queen Victoria, 1837 to 1901. Absolutely right. So the scores at the end of round one, Diana, are?
Diana:	At the end of round 1, Bob, Peter has scored 30 but his wife,

	Jenny, has scored 40 points!
Questioner:	Right, on to round two. Peter, some catching up to do here. Now, Peter has a bell in front of him and Jenny has a buzzer. Can we just hear those to check that they're working? Jenny. (*Buzz*) Lovely. And Peter, let's hear your bell. (*Ring*) Wonderful. Right, now, I'm going to ask questions about the geography of Great Britain. The first person to press his bell or her buzzer gets to answer the question. If it's wrong, I'll hand it over to the other person. OK? And as before, there are ten points for each correct answer. Here we go then with the first question in round two. Which is the longest river in Britain? Jenny.
Jenny:	Thames?
Questioner:	I'm afraid not. Not the Thames, no. Peter?
Peter:	The Severn?
Questioner:	Absolutely right. More by luck than judgement I suspect, but nevertheless the Severn is correct, 220 miles of it. Right, ready for question two. Which is the highest mountain in Britain?
Questioner:	Jenny.
Jenny:	Ben Nevis.
Questioner:	Absolutely right. Ben Nevis in Scotland. Right, question three, level pegging for round two so far. Question three is name two of the seas or oceans that surround Britain.
Questioner:	Jenny again.
Jenny:	North Sea and Irish Sea.
Questioner:	The North Sea and the Irish Sea. Correct! The other two were the Atlantic or the English Channel, but those two are fine. Right, Jenny's steaming ahead again here. Question four, how many cities in England have more than one million inhabitants?
Questioner:	Peter.
Peter:	Four.
Questioner:	I'm afraid not. Jenny?
Jenny:	I really don't know.
Questioner:	Well, all right, the answer is in fact three. Greater London, Greater Manchester and Birmingham. No score for question four. Question five. Name the capital cities of the four countries in the United Kingdom.
Questioner:	Jenny.
Jenny:	Edinburgh, Cardiff, London and . . . Belfast.
Questioner:	Absolutely correct. All right, moving right along now to question six. Name two of London's main airports.
Questioner:	Oh, very quick, I think the buzzer just had it. Jenny?
Peter:	I don't think so, Bob!
Questioner:	I can see he must get tricky over the washing up at home!
Jenny:	Yes, he does. I think I was first!
Questioner:	All right, all right. Let's have Jenny's answer. Two of London's main airports.
Jenny:	Heathrow and Gatwick.
Questioner:	Absolutely right, the other would have been Stanstead. Yes, all right, you know the other one as well. Right, question seven, Peter. You've got two questions to catch up here. I'm *sure* you can do it. What is the name of the mountain range that divides the east of England from the west?
Questioner:	Oh, Jenny, you're too fast . . . Yes?
Jenny:	Pennines.
Questioner:	The Pennines it is! Right, there's no stopping her, is there?

Question eight, Peter. Come on, we're all rooting for you now. Which is the largest lake in England?

Questioner: Peter.

Peter: Windermere.

Questioner: Absolutely correct Peter, Windermere. And the score at the end of round two. Diana, is . . .?

Diana: Well, Bob, the score at the end of round two is . . . Peter has now got 50 points but Jenny has got an *amazing* 40, 50, 60, 70, 80, 90 points!

UNIT 3

A village walk
(page 46)

Welcome to Ditchling. I'm sure that you will enjoy your walk around the village as you listen to this cassette. Every so often you will hear this sound (*Beep*). This means that you should switch off the cassette, and leave it switched off until you reach the last place mentioned. Our starting point is the Village Hall, built on the site of a school which was burnt down in 1919. As you walk towards the centre of the village, notice the old oak door on your left in the sixteenth-century house called Tudor Close. This is now part of Ditchling Press. Carry on along this road until you get to the crossroads.

(*Beep*)

When you come to the crossroads, you will see opposite you an antique shop which is another sixteenth-century house. If you look down South Street, the road that leads to Brighton, you can see The Jointure on the right; this is the house where Frank Brangwyn, the famous artist, lived. Now cross the busy road with the High Street on your right and walk up the slope towards the church. Beneath West Street there is a series of large cellars which were once connected to each other. They were used by the smugglers who frequently passed through the village. When you reach the White Horse Inn, cross the road and climb the steps to the church.

(*Beep*)

You should now be standing outside the church. Look back across the road to Wings Place, a superb seventeenth-century house. Now take the path across the Green, turn right up Lodge Hill Lane and stop by the pond with its ducks and moorhens. You will see the school on the further bank.

(*Beep*)

In front of you, you should now see Lodge Hill, on top of which is an ancient burial mound. At the foot of the hill runs the Roman road straight as a die from Streat in the east to Hassocks in the west. Turn left up the hill along the oldest lane in the village, and then pause at the gate in the bend in the road to enjoy a wide view across the fields to Keymer.

(*Beep*)

The footpath which runs straight on from here indicates the line of the Roman road we mentioned earlier. Carry on up the road until you reach the old mill, which was last used in 1918.

(*Beep*)

Now go back towards the village and turn left along Boddingtons Lane, until it leads you to the upper part of the High Street.

(*Beep*)

You should now see opposite you a house with two flights of steps let into the wall. The further flight leads to the front door of the house, while the nearer one used to lead to the stable door of a saddler's shop. If you look carefully you can still see the iron ring in the wall used for tying horses, and a piece of wood sticking out by the window (where the door used to be) for holding a saddle. As you start to walk down the High Street, notice the delightful view of the distant hills, with Ditchling

Beacon the highest point. In the days of Queen Elizabeth I the bonfire lit on this beacon was a warning that the Spanish Armada was sailing up the English Channel. Just before you reach the crossroads, you will pass the Bull Inn on the left-hand side. Turn left into Lewes Road, and you will see the Village Hall again on your right.

(Beep)

I hope very much that you have enjoyed this brief walk around Ditchling, and thank you for showing interest in our village. Please return this cassette and cassette player to the attendant, who will refund your deposit. Thank you and goodbye.

UNIT 4

Flight information (page 63)

Good morning, ladies and gentlemen, and welcome on board this Royal Airlines flight to Rome with Captain Peters in command. Our flight time will be two hours and ten minutes, and we shall be cruising at an altitude of 29,000 feet. Our estimated time of arrival is 12.45 local time.

Please ensure that your seatbelt is securely fastened, and refrain from smoking until we are airborne and the no-smoking signs have been switched off. All seatbacks and tables must be placed in the fully upright position in preparation for take-off.

In the seat pocket you will find the Flight Safety Card showing safety procedures for this aircraft. Notice how to operate the quick-release buckle fitted to your seatbelt. (Pause) Routes to all exits are clearly marked. Cabin crew will now point out the nearest exits in your area.

During the flight, the air in the cabin is carefully controlled for your safety and comfort. Should supplementary oxygen be required at any time, oxygen masks like this will automatically drop down from the overhead panels. If this happens, you must remain seated, pull the mask down like this and place it over your nose and mouth and breathe normally. It is the action of pulling down the mask that activates the oxygen supply. All smoking material should be extinguished immediately, as smoking is not permitted when oxygen is in use. For your information, it is normal in such circumstances for the aircraft to commence an immediate controlled descent.

Your life-jacket is stowed in a packet beneath your seat. Ladies and gentlemen, thank you for your attention, and we wish you a very pleasant flight. Thank you.

UNIT 5

Radio programme (page 75)

Graham:	Welcome to *At Your Service*, the consumer programme that gives you advice when something goes wrong with goods or services you've bought. If you have a problem which you'd like us to help you with, here's the number to ring: 01-246 8041. That's 01-246 8041. My name is Graham Mills, and with me to answer your questions today is the chairman of the Consumer Aid Association, Pauline Duffy. Good morning, Pauline.
Pauline:	Good morning, Graham.
Graham:	Right, let's go straight to our first caller who is Mr Somerset from Nottingham. Good morning, Mr Somerset.
Mr Somerset:	Oh, good morning.
Graham:	And how can we help you?
Mr Somerset:	Well, if I can speak to Mrs Duffy . . .?
Graham:	Yes, she's listening.
Mr Somerset:	Well, I was looking for a second-hand car and I saw this advert in the local paper and it was the sort of car I wanted and it was the right sort of price. It was £1,150 and it was

described as immaculate so I thought that would do me. So I went to see the man and it looked . . . it looked very good so I bought it. Oh, I didn't . . . I had a look at it, but I mean I'm not a . . . mechanic or anything so I, you know, I just bought it. Anyway . . .

Pauline:	Mr Somerset, could I interrupt?
Mr Somerset:	Yes, please.
Pauline:	Did you pay the full asking price for the car?
Mr Somerset:	Yes, yes, I paid £1,150 for it . . . and it seemed all right and I got it home and then, a few days later, I had some trouble starting it, and it . . . well . . . from then on things sort of went wrong. It was difficult to start and when it was started, it didn't run very well, it was uneven running and not firing properly. So anyway I took it to my local garage . . . Well, they had a good look at it and they said it was terrible. It was . . . everything was wrong with it really . . . and it had been damaged in an accident and the repairs hadn't been very good, they'd been very bad . . . so it wasn't worth the money I'd paid for it. In fact, *they* said it was only worth about £400 . . . Well, that was, you know, I said to them what would it cost to put it right and they said maybe £250 and even then I . . . well it would probably only be worth they said, I think they said, £750. Well, that's a lot less than I'd paid for it and that's if I paid another £250. So I went back to the man I bought it from, but he didn't really want to know and I don't know what to do now. I've really sort of lost a lot of money.
Pauline:	Mr Somerset, you have in fact been in touch with the man that you bought the car from?
Mr Somerset:	Yeah, well, I went back to see him, but, I mean, he didn't really . . . he didn't really want to talk to me at all about it.
Pauline:	The most important point here, Mr Somerset, I think is . . . was the seller a dealer or was this a private sale?
Mr Somerset:	I don't think he was a dealer. I mean, it was a private house I went to and it seemed to be . . . it was just standing in the road outside his house so, I mean, I couldn't . . .
Pauline:	Well, unfortunately, with private sales the buyer has, under the law, very little protection. You *may* have a claim if the man that you bought the car from made a statement about the car which persuaded you to buy the car and on which you relied, but that statement later turned out to be false and this would seem to be absolutely the case here.
Mr Somerset:	Yeah, he did say . . . I mean, in the advert it said 'immaculate'. I mean, that was actually in the paper.
Pauline:	And that was a word which tempted you to buy the car, presumably?
Mr Somerset:	Yes, yeah.
Pauline:	When you bought the car you bought it understanding that it was faultless, that there was nothing wrong with it at all?
Mr Somerset:	Yeah, he didn't say there was anything wrong and I said, you know, does it run well and that and he said, no, it was in very good condition.
Pauline:	I'm sorry to be slightly pessimistic about this, Mr Somerset, it's . . . I think it's probably worthwhile you making a claim under the Small Claims Procedure of the County Court. That is the best avenue for you but, as I say, with private sales it's a very difficult area and one really couldn't guarantee the outcome. But I think you'll find that the Small Claims Procedure of the County Court is your . . .

Mr Somerset: your best bet.
I see. Yeah, well, thank you very much. I'll . . . I'll . . .

Graham: Thank you, Mr Somerset. Thank you very much for your call and I hope that's been of some help to you. We'll move on now to our second caller of the morning . . .

UNIT 6

**Do it yourself
(page 87)**

I can't deal with what I've got.
Her kind of love is thanks a lot.
You all think we're happy
I'm telling you we're not.
I can't deal with what I've got.

I used to have such a simple life
Just working 8 till 5.
She's got me out there now all the time
Trying to keep us both alive.
All her fancy leather shoes
And all that make-up that she use,
If she don't hand me out some clues,
Oh lady! We're both gonna lose.

I can't deal with what I've got.
Her kind of love is thanks a lot.
You think I'm happy,
I'm telling you I'm not.
I can't deal with what I've got.

When I come home the oven's always cold,
Your kind of cooking's making me old.
So where did you get that tan?
Come on, sugar, won't you open a can?
You're my woman, I'm your man.
Oh lady! We're both gonna lose.

And now she says, she says
Do it yourself, do it yourself.
That's what she says, she says
Do it yourself, do it yourself.

We're both gonna lose.

Now she says, she says . . .

Somebody help me, please.

UNIT 7

**Listening to the news
(page 104)**

The time is nine o'clock this Monday morning, and here is your local news for the south-east.

Reports of casualties are still coming in from the car ferry that capsized just outside Dover last night. The ferry was leaving the harbour on its way to Calais with 517 people on board, when it apparently crashed into the harbour wall and turned quickly over on to its side, trapping most of the passengers and crew inside. So far, over 340 survivors have been picked up from the icy waters, but we have not received any definite details of the number known to have died. We will, of course, keep you up-to-date just as soon as we receive any further information.

Police have still not been able to identify the man who was found shot on Brighton beach on Saturday evening. He's described as in his mid-thirties, six-foot tall, overweight, with thick fair hair, and wearing a dark suit. A police spokesman said this morning that there was no evidence that any other person had been involved.

In Shoreham, a row has broken out over a proposed new road to take heavy traffic away from the town centre. Many local residents fear their homes will be demolished, though town planning officials have denied that this will be the case.

In Hastings, teachers have voted to strike in support of a colleague who was sacked last week for refusing to teach a class of 13-year-olds he described as 'criminal savages'. The sacked teacher, Mr George Mansfield, told the Education Board last week that he would return to his class when the children apologised and showed that they could behave in a civilized manner.

The South East Courier, one of the south-east's longest established newspapers, is in dificulties following the decision by a chain of estate agents to transfer its advertising to one of the new free weekly newspapers. A spokesman for Jones and Wainright, the estate agents with branches throughout the south-east, said, 'This is not a step we have taken lightly, but, like everyone else, we have to move with the times.'

And now for the weather. Today will be mostly sunny, with temperatures in the upper forties Fahrenheit, that's about 9 degrees Celsius, though there may be some cloud and light showers later on in the day. And that's all from me for now. I'll be back at twelve o'clock with more local news.

UNIT 8

**Radio programme:
Witness (page 114)**

Peter: Welcome to *Witness*, the programme where *you* can help us solve crimes and find the criminals. If you recognise any of the stolen goods we describe, or any of the criminals we're looking for, give us a ring on this number, 01-246 8007, and detectives will be waiting to take down your information. Or, if you prefer, you can talk to one of our specially trained radio staff. In either case, you are guaranteed complete anonymity. You have no need to fear that your name will be passed on to anyone else or that you yourself might be exposed to any danger. Sue.

Sue: Yes. Well, Peter, we're going to start off by describing some rather nice items of jewellery that have been recovered in different parts of the country in the last few weeks. Now, we *do* know that all these items were stolen but we don't know exactly where or when and, of course, we don't know *who* stole them. So, if you recognise any of the descriptions, either because the jewellery is yours, or because you've seen it somewhere else, please do phone us immediately. Now, the first object is a rather lovely five-stone ring. It's a modern design. It has two diamonds and three sapphires and its maximum value is two thousand pounds. The ring has an eighth-of-an-inch gold band. And here's a clue which *must* ring a bell with someone listening. It has initials engraved on the band and the initials are W.E.Z . . . unusual initials those.

The next item is a double row of pearls. Its value is around four-and-a-half thousand pounds. They're a normal necklace length and they have a diamond clasp. That's a double row of large pearls.

And the last item is a gold lady's watch. It has a safety chain attached. Its value is around five hundred pounds. The watch has a half-inch square black face and there's a hallmark on it which tells us it was made in 1972 and it's a Swiss watch. So someone at home must be missing those items and I hope may recognise them. Now it's back to you, Peter.

Peter: Thank you, Sue.

Well, did *you* recognise any of those items? If so, remember the number to ring is, 01 (if you live outside London) 246 8007, that's 01-246 8007 . . .

UNIT 9

Signals used by referees and linesman (page 131)

Course Tutor: Right. Now then. Now, you've all come on this course for referees and linesmen, so I – or I suppose I should say 'linespersons', should I? – so I expect you've all watched quite a lot of football. *But,* I wonder if you've ever paid much attention to the signals that referees and linesmen give? I mean, now, they're not very complicated, but, of course, it's vital that they're used in the correct manner so that all the people involved in the game – the players *and* the officials – know exactly what's going on. So, I want to start off by seeing how much you already know about these signals. Now, for instance, does anyone know what signal to give if the referee wants play to continue – that's to say, if he doesn't want play to stop?

Woman 1: Er, doesn't he put his hands forward, like this?

Course Tutor: Yes. Yes, that's right. The arms are held forwards, at waist height, with the palms upwards. That's good. And, can anyone tell me what *this* signal means: when I blow my whistle and point with the other hand down towards the ground?

Man 1: Some sort of free kick, isn't it?

Course Tutor: Yes, that's right. It is. What sort of a free kick is it, though?

Man 2: Direct. Direct free kick.

Course Tutor: That's right. That's right. A direct free kick. So, in that case, what is the signal for an *in*direct free kick?

Woman 2: Oh . . .

Course Tutor: Yes?

Woman 2: It's one palm raised up, and one down.

Course Tutor: That's right – one hand held firmly beside . . . down at the side, and the right hand held straight up in the air.

Man 2: Palm up.

Course Tutor: That's right. That's an indirect free kick. Good. Well now, going on to linesmen. What would a linesman do if he saw a foul?

Man 1: Put his flag up.

Course Tutor: Yes . . .

Woman 2: Yeah, but, but . . . held right up.

Course Tutor: Yeah. Anything else? Does more than just . . .?

Woman 2: Wave it about – backwards and forwards.

Course Tutor: That's . . . yes. Now that *is* important. He waves it about, but he waves it backwards and forwards. The object, of course, is to catch the referee's eye, so the movement is more likely to catch the eye. That's why that signal is the way it is. Excellent! . . .

Man 3: Excuse me . . .

Course Tutor: Yes?

Man 3: Doesn't it depend where the foul is?

Course Tutor: Ah, well . . . yes. That's perfectly right, because if the foul is in the penalty area – if you obviously know the difference – you can tell me what the signal is.

Man 3:	Well, the linesman holds the flag across his body.
Course Tutor:	Yes. That's right. He holds it across his body, up towards his shoulder. Now . . . another of the linesman's signals: what would he signal if he sees a player offside?
Man 3:	I used to know that.
Woman 2:	Isn't it when he holds it straight out in front of him? He's got the . . .
Course Tutor:	That's right, that's right. Holding the flag straight out across the line of play in the direction in which the offside took place. Fair enough. Now then, moving back to referees for a moment, what does this signal mean – if the referee holds his hands up, palms outwards, in front of his chest?
Man 1:	That's when he . . . That's when he wants a new ball, isn't it?
Course Tutor:	That's right, yes. He actually looks as though he's asking for the ball to be put in his hands. So, that's good. Right now, then – there's another signal that linesmen give. A linesman standing with the flag straight down by his right hand side and his hand in front of his thigh with two fingers pointing downwards, flat against his leg.
Woman 1:	Ti . . . Oh! . . .
Course Tutor:	What does that mean?
Woman 1:	Time up?
Course Tutor:	No, not time up. He's got two fingers pointing downwards.
Woman 1:	Two . . . two minutes until . . .
Course Tutor:	Two minutes . . .
Woman 1:	. . . till the end of the match.
Course Tutor:	Till the end of the match, according to his timing. That's right. He's indicating to the referee . . .

UNIT 10

**Keep warm
(page 146)**

Robin:	Good morning, and welcome to our *Keep Warm* series. It really is a terrible problem for many people to keep warm during this awful, freezing-cold weather, so every day we give you tips on how to keep your body temperature up. Nothing too strenuous, mind you. We try to keep it simple – and fun. Paula, what have you got for us today?
Paula:	Well, I've been looking at a very easy warm-up routine that anybody can use in the mornings to get the old blood circulation going. Would you like to try it with me, Robin?
Robin:	Oh . . . well, all right, if you insist.
Paula:	Just think how amazingly fit and healthy *and* warm you're going to be after doing this each morning before setting out to face the elements. Right are you ready listeners?
	Start by running on the spot gently, checking that your toes are pointing downwards in best ballet style. Now gradually try to get your knees higher and higher until you're actually running on the spot. Do this for at least one minute (we'll pretend a minute's gone now) and then give yourself a well-earned rest by bending your body over in a floppy-doll stance, and r-e-l-a-x. Well done.
	OK, now before you relax too much, get ready for the next part of winter warm-ups. Now these are going to be scissor-jumps. Stand still with your legs and feet smartly together, hands by your side. Now, spread your legs wide apart by jumping into the air and at the same time bring your arms up and over your head and clap them together. Have another jump to bring the legs back

into a closed position with the arms once again at your side. OK, let's start. We'll do a few of these jumps to start with, and then later on you can work up to do twenty or so at one time. Now make sure you start gently and, until you feel able to do it with ease, and without huffing and puffing too much, like Robin. Well, we'll be coming back a bit later on in the programme to practise these exercises again. You can stop now, Robin.

Robin: Thank goodness for that. Oh . . . a bit too energetic for me, Paula, I'm afraid. But I must admit, I'm warm. Well now, let's hear from Dr Henderson, who's got some advice about a slightly less exhausting way of getting warm.

UNIT 11

Treating shock (page 158)

Right, tonight we're going to look at the problem of shock. In medical terms, shock isn't just emotional upset. It is a very definite physical condition in which the heart and the circulation gradually lose power. Gradually the patient becomes pale and cold, drowsy, and perhaps he or she even loses consciousness. Shock can result from all major injuries – bleeding, wounds, burns and fractures – and the speed of the patient's deterioration depends on the severity of the damage. So, whenever someone has been badly injured, you must do *two* things: you must give specific help for the actual injury itself, and you must also do something to halt or at least to try and reduce the shock process. Now here's one or two hints on how to do this.

First of all, you mustn't move the patient unless you absolutely have to. If you're in a burning house or in the middle of a motorway, you'll have to move him, of course. But otherwise treat him where he is until the doctor or the ambulance arrives. And the next thing to remember is that you should position the patient lying down with his head low and his feet raised. This is to help the blood flow to the heart, lungs and brain. But don't, of course, be tempted to move any part that might be fractured. Be careful always of that. Loosen any tight clothing, such as braces, belt, collar or even – you'll be surprised to learn nowadays – corsets. This will make the patient more comfortable and allow him to breathe more easily.

Keep the patient warm by laying a blanket or coat loosely over them. If he's lying on a cold surface, then try to put something underneath him as well. But again, do that very gently. *Don't* use hot-water bottles, because hot-water bottles actually draw blood away from the internal organs towards the skin surface. So, although that may sound like a commonsense thing to do, it actually isn't.

Reassure the patient, this is very important, by being calm yourself, confident, methodical and, above everything, sympathetic the whole time. Even if the patient seems to be unconscious, they may be able to hear any unfavourable comments you make, in actual fact. And if he hears or sees you whispering, then he's bound to imagine the worst. He'll be in a very frightened state and this will make his condition worse too.

And the final point to remember is that you must *not* give anything at all by mouth. Any sort of drink, whether alcohol or tea or coffee, may be vomited up, causing choking. And it may also complicate matters if an anaesthetic is needed later in hospital. So, all the old wive's tales you've heard about administering brandy, forget them. If the patient feels dry and he says he's thirsty, or you suspect that they may be thirsty, you can allow him to suck gently a cloth or a sponge moistened with water.

Well now, let's see if you can put all this into practice . . . I think Peter, you can be the victim and, Richard, I think you'll be a very competent and, I'm sure, sympathetic First Aider.

'Girl number twenty', said Mr Gradgrind, squarely pointing with his square forefinger, 'I don't know that girl. Who is that girl?'

'Sissy Jupe, sir,' explained number twenty, blushing, standing up, and curtseying.

'Sissy is not a name,' said Mr Gradgrind. 'Don't call yourself Sissy. Call yourself Cecilia.'

'It's father as calls me Sissy, sir,' returned the young girl in a trembling voice, and with another curtsey.

'Then he has no business to do it,' said Mr Gradgrind. 'Tell him he mustn't. Cecilia Jupe. Let me see. What is your father?'

'He belongs to the horse-riding, if you please, sir.'

Mr Gradgrind frowned, and waved off the objectionable calling with his hand.

'We don't want to know anything about that, here. You mustn't tell us about that, here. Your father breaks horses, doesn't he?'

'If you please, sir, when they can get any to break, they do break horses in the ring, sir.'

'You mustn't tell us about the ring, here. Very well, then. Describe your father as a horsebreaker. He doctors sick horses, I dare say?'

'Oh yes, sir.'

'Very well then. He is a veterinary surgeon, a farrier and horse-breaker. Give me your definition of a horse.'

(Sissy Jupe thrown into the greatest alarm by this demand.)

'Girl number twenty unable to define a horse!' said Mr Gradgrind . . . 'Girl number twenty possessed of no facts, in reference to one of the commonest of animals! Some boy's definition of a horse. Bitzer, yours.'

The square finger, moving here and there, lighted suddenly on Bitzer, perhaps because he chanced to sit in the same ray of sunlight which, darting in at one of the bare windows of the intensely white-washed room, irradiated Sissy. For, the boys and girls sat on the face of the inclined plane in two compact bodies, divided up the centre by a narrow interval; and Sissy, being at the corner of a row on the sunny side, came in for the beginning of a sunbeam, of which Bitzer, being at the corner of a row on the other side, a few rows in advance, caught the end. But, whereas the girl was so dark-eyed and dark-haired, that she seemed to receive a deeper and more lustrous colour from the sun when it shone upon her, the boy was so light-eyed and light-haired that the self-same rays appeared to draw out of him what little colour he ever possessed. His cold eyes would hardly have been eyes, but for the short ends of lashes which, by bringing them into immediate contrast with something paler than themselves, expressed their form. His short-cropped hair might have been a mere continuation of the sandy freckles on his forehead and face. His skin was so unwholesomely deficient in the natural tinge, that he looked as though, if he were cut, he would bleed white.

'Bitzer', said Thomas Gradgrind. 'Your definition of a horse.'

'Quadruped. Graminivorous. Forty teeth, namely twenty-four grinders, four eye-teeth, and twelve incisive. Sheds coat in the spring; in marshy countries, sheds hoofs, too. Hoofs hard, but requiring to be shod with iron. Age known by marks in mouth.' Thus (and much more) Bitzer.

'Now girl number twenty,' said Mr Gradgrind. 'You know what a horse is.'

APPENDIX

Irregular Verbs

Infinitive	Past tense	Past participle
arise	arose	arisen
awake	awoke	awoken, awaked
be (am, is , are)	was, were	been
bear	bore	borne
beat	beat	beaten
become	became	become
begin	began	begun
bend	bent	bent
bet	bet	bet
bid	bid	bid
bind	bound	bound
bite	bit	bitten
bleed	bled	bled
blow	blew	blown
break	broke	broken
breed	bred	bred
bring	brought	brought
broadcast	broadcast	broadcast
build	built	built
burn	burnt, burned	burnt, burned
burst	burst	burst
buy	bought	bought
cast	cast	cast
catch	caught	caught
choose	chose	chosen
cling	clung	clung
come	came	come
cost	cost	cost
creep	crept	crept
cut	cut	cut
deal	dealt	dealt
dig	dug	dug
do	did	done
draw	drew	drawn
dream	dreamt, dreamed	dreamt, dreamed
drink	drank	drunk
drive	drove	driven
eat	ate	eaten
fall	fell	fallen
feed	fed	fed
feel	felt	felt
fight	fought	fought
find	found	found
flee	fled	fled
fling	flung	flung
fly	flew	flown
forbid	forbade, forbad	forbidden
forecast	forecast	forecast
forget	forgot	forgotten
forgive	forgave	forgiven
freeze	froze	frozen
get	got	got (USA gotten)
give	gave	given
go	went	gone
grind	ground	ground
grow	grew	grown
hang	hung, hanged	hung, hanged

APPENDIX

Infinitive	Past tense	Past participle	Infinitive	Past tense	Past participle
have (has)	had	had	sing	sang	sung
hear	heard	heard	sink	sank	sunk; sunken
hide	hid	hidden	sit	sat	sat
hit	hit	hit	slay	slew	slain
hold	held	held	sleep	slept	slept
hurt	hurt	hurt	slide	slid	slid
keep	kept	kept	slit	slit	slit
kneel	knelt	knelt	smell	smelt, smelled	smelt, smelled
know	knew	known	sow	sowed	sown, sowed
lay	laid	laid	speak	spoke	spoken
lead	led	led	speed	sped	sped
lean	leant, leaned	leant, leaned	spell	spelt, spelled	spelt, spelled
leap	leapt, leaped	leapt, leaped	spend	spent	spent
learn	learnt, learned	learnt, learned	spill	spilt, spilled	spilt, spilled
leave	left	left	spin	spun, span	spun
lend	lent	lent	spit	spat, (USA spit)	spat, (USA spit)
let	let	let	split	split	split
lie	lay	lain	spoil	spoilt, spoiled	spoilt, spoiled
light	lit	lit	spread	spread	spread
lose	lost	lost	spring	sprang	sprung
make	made	made	stand	stood	stood
mean	meant	meant	steal	stole	stolen
meet	met	met	stick	stuck	stuck
mistake	mistook	mistaken	sting	stung	stung
misunderstand	misunderstood	misunderstood	stink	stank, stunk	stunk
pay	paid	paid	strike	struck	struck, stricken
put	put	put	swear	swore	sworn
read	read	read	sweep	swept	swept
ride	rode	ridden	swim	swam	swum
ring	rang, rung	rung	swing	swung	swung
rise	rose	risen	take	took	taken
run	ran	run	teach	taught	taught
saw	sawed	sawn, sawed	tear	tore	torn
say	said	said	tell	told	told
see	saw	seen	think	thought	thought
seek	sought	sought	throw	threw	thrown
sell	sold	sold	thrust	thrust	thrust
send	sent	sent	tread	trod	trodden, trod
set	set	set	upset	upset	upset
sew	sewed	sewn, sewed	wake	woke	woken
shake	shook	shaken	wear	wore	worn
shine	shone	shone	weave	wove	woven
shoot	shot	shot	weep	wept	wept
show	showed	shown, showed	win	won	won
shrink	shrank	shrunk	wind	wound	wound
shut	shut	shut	write	wrote	written

INDEX